Under the

Stained Glass Ceiling

Sexual Harassment of United Methodist

Clergywomen by Laity

Beth A. Cooper

Sexual harassment remains a problem

within The United Methodist Church

and laity need more education about the issue.

Linda Bloom
United Methodist News Service
September 20, 2005

Praise for

Under the Stained Glass Ceiling

I want to affirm the importance of the research and analysis represented here. Beth Cooper does a very good job of laying out the complexities and difficulties faced by women clergy who experience sexual harassment from laity, the harm this does not only to women clergy but to the church as a whole. I was particularly impressed with the discussion regarding the difficulties of responding to lay harassment within a volunteer organization. This is surely a major factor in the church's inadequate response to this problem. How to discipline someone whose role in relation to church structures is basically voluntary is a real challenge with no easy answers.

Dr. Cooper's proposals for greater education seem to me to be right on the mark as the most useful means of bringing the church to a greater level of responsibility in dealing with gender issues in general, as well as sexual harassment as a particular form of gender bias. Her combination of statistical reporting and personal interviews with women clergy provides the reader with both the broad context and the personal cost of this behavior.

This is important research that has significance not only for the United Methodist Church. Other denominations would do well to consider their own response to harassment of clergy women by laity. While its focus is on one US denomination, it would be foolish for non-Methodist readers to assume that their clergywomen do not experience any such problems. They too can learn from this work. This study shines a light on an aspect of church life that is rarely acknowledged and, when it is acknowledged, it is often inadequately dealt with by church leaders.

Dr. Marjorie Procter-Smith
LeVan Professor of Christian Worship
Perkins School of Theology
Southern Methodist University, Dallas, TX

The Rev. Dr. Beth Cooper has pulled back the curtain on a problem facing women clergy as long as women have been clergy--sexual harassment and violence from church members. With powerful and painful stories, solid research and substantive recommendations, Rev. Cooper's book will change the way ministry is implemented and managed in the entire United Methodist Church.

J. Ann Craig *Communications Consultant, New York*
United Methodists layperson,
Former Executive Director for Spiritual and Theological Development
Women's Division, The United Methodist Church

The Rev. Dr. Beth Cooper has prophetic imagination to name the wrong of the abuse of clergywomen by laity, and even more prophetic imagination to envision the corrections of polity, policy and life together for faithful congregation where men and women alike live out their callings in fruitful and enduring ways.

Dr. Lewis A. Parks *Director, Doctor of Ministry Program*
Professor of Theology, Ministry, and Congregational Development
Wesley Theological Seminary, Washington, DC

When parishioners know no boundaries in regards to the personal lives of clergywomen, they are more likely to set up an environment where someone can take advantage of the fact that no one will believe, help or advocate for the clergywoman.

Bishop Sally Dyck
Minnesota Area
The United Methodist Church

As the body of Christ, we must live out a theology that honors the fully embodied clergy leadership of women in the church with institutional practices that prevent sexual harassment from occurring in the first place and has no tolerance for it when it does occur.

The Rev. Dr. Traci C. West
Professor of Ethics and African American Studies
Drew Theological School, Madison, NJ

Under the

Stained Glass Ceiling

Sexual Harassment of United Methodist

Clergywomen by Laity

Beth A. Cooper, M.Div., D.Min.

Frontrowliving Press
PO Box 19291
San Diego, CA 92159
619-955-0925
frontrowliving@yahoo.com

Under the Stained Glass Ceiling:
Sexual Harassment of United Methodist Clergywomen by Laity

Quotations from *The Book of Discipline* and *The Book of Resolutions of The United Methodist Church* are used with permission from The United Methodist Publishing House, Nashville, Tennessee.

Quotations from Carol Becker's book, *Leading Women: How Church Women Can Avoid Leadership Traps and Negotiate the Gender Maze*, are used with permission from Abingdon Press, Nashville, Tennessee.

The cover photo is a watercolor painting of St. Giles Cathedral, Edinburgh, Scotland, 1884, unsigned.

Book and cover design by Frontrowliving Press.

Manufactured in the United States of America

ISBN 978-0-9794194-3-0

Dedication

To my mother, The Rev. Elizabeth S. Cooper

For all the women who dare to boldly answer their call to ministry in the church, out of the church, and beyond the church. Thank you for your witness.

For the lay persons who have grown beyond cultural norms and family systems of oppression, thank you for your witness.

The journey is truly about recognizing the Christ in all of us. I believe someone needs to shout it to the church rafters, to break the glass ceiling!

The journey goes on. Until we meet, the spirit of Christ be with you. Let it be. Amen.

Contents

Acknowledgments

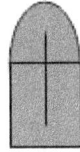

Thank you for reading this book. I hope that it adds to your awareness and that you will help inspire the church to do the right thing and adequately deal with clergywomen when laity harass them. I invite you to be a part of that change. This has been a decade long endeavor that grew out of God's call. I challenge the church that nurtured and ordained me to do better, and in doing so, to reach those who desire to be disciples of Jesus Christ.

I spoke with theologians, professors, lay people and church leaders of several different denominations. I interviewed over three hundred clergywomen and spoke at length with clergywomen who, for their healing process, needed to be heard. I thank the clergywomen who found their way to me and shared their stories.

Many people have helped make this book possible. I especially thank the Women Studies Department, Humans Research Committee, and the Social Science Department of San Diego State University. I also want to thank Dr. Lewis Parks and Wesley Theological Seminary in Washington DC, and Dr. Marjorie Procter-Smith of Perkins School of Theology.

I would like to thank family and friends, especially my mother, The Rev. Elizabeth Stanton Cooper, Barbara Mesol, Dr. Monica Murphy and The Rev. Dr. Alice Knotts, my editor. Dr. Traci C. West, Ann Craig, The Rev. Alice Ann Glenn, and Bishop Sally Dyck made excellent suggestions and contributions. Thank you all for your witness.

Preface

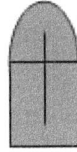

The Rev. Dr. Traci C. West

"I know. I know. One time a kid in my church said something like that to me, too," one of my colleagues said. Then he joined the laughter of others in our clergy group. They were responding to a story someone had just shared. This was a welcome moment of levity during the coffee break at a boring, all day United Methodist District clergy meeting,. The friendly laughter arose in response to one colleague's story about a pastoral call to a parishioner's home. A child opened the front door and greeted him by shouting up the stairs: "Mom, God's here."

I tried to hide my surprise at the nodding, smiling agreement within this group of white male clergy colleagues. Their reactions to the incident as a familiar, quite ordinary occurrence amazed me. As a twenty-five year old, African American female pastor, the story did not at all resonate with visceral reactions to me by either adult or child parishioners in the congregation I served. Though the vivid memory stays with me, this moment of dissonance with my male colleagues occurred many years ago, shortly after I had just started serving in full-time pastoral ministry.

God. Sex/Gender. Power. They are all bound-up together in Christian biblical and theological images of what authoritative leadership looks like. Through some of its most important rituals conferring status in the Christian faith community, the church teaches us to link male gender and sexuality to the potent, divine power of God. In the Sacrament of Baptism, a ritual required for all members of the Christian faith community, the church mandates the invocation of God the Father by the presiding ordained pastor when blessing the child (or adult) to signify an unbreakable, Divine covenant with her or him. It is again the authority of God the Father, not to be replaced with names such as Triune God and certainly not Mother-Father God, that episcopal leaders must ritually invoke to bless each ordinand, marking their entrance into clergy membership.

If femaleness is mentioned in the intertwined themes of God, sex/gender, and power that are included in our Christian tradition, too often condemnation or censure is attached to it. The metaphorical violence in scriptural theology offers especially troubling examples. In the book of Ezekiel, for instance, Jerusalem, imaged as an adulterous wife is described as "a whore" that God must uncover before a mob "so that they may see all your nakedness" (Ezekiel 16:37), stone her, and cut to her pieces with swords. In the New Testament book of Revelation "the great whore" must be made "desolate and naked" and then her flesh devoured and burnt (Revelation 17:17) in the apocalyptic images God inspires. No references to any such violence appear in New Testament passages about women's church leadership. In scripture frequently utilized to justify barring women from ordination and rejecting their leadership in any capacity in the church, it states: "I permit no woman to teach or have authority over a man; she is to keep silent" (1Timothy 2.11). In fact, God's salvation is still possible according to this Pauline text, but only "through childbearing, provided they continue in faith and love and holiness, with modesty" (1Timothy 2.15). It is within a Christian cultural context informed by theological and biblical ideas such as these that the sexual harassment of clergywomen occurs.

We need to take an inventory of all the Christian theological and biblical messages about gender, sex, authority, power, and God undergirding our beliefs and church practices to fully understand why the sexual harassment of clergywomen persists and how to address it. Which biblical interpretations and theological claims help us to recognize sexual harassment of clergywomen as harmful? Which ones support our tolerance for sexual harassment of clergywomen?

Christian theology about sex, gender, and power is not produced in a religious bubble. The perceptions we bring to this study of sexual harassment include broader cultural influences from current trends in the media and politics as well as influences from varied, ancient cultural contexts that inform scripture. Our understanding of sex, gender, and power in the church arise from an amalgam of secular and Christian religious sources that *collectively* shape our openness to learning from this study. Since the topic of sexual harassment is so intensely political (concerned with power), each of our distinctive experiences of the politics of community life matter. They also impact our openness to study it. We are influenced by our experience of white racism, the class privileges of higher education, or exclusion from a beloved church family because of heterosexist policies. Therefore we may bring certain preconceptions about the seriousness of sexual harassment. We may be convinced that clergywomen's authority is already regarded as equal to their male peers, or simply be unsure about how much significance stopping sexual harassment of women clergy (or laity) has for the broad mission and ministry of the church.

This study offers an opportunity to examine those preconceptions. The detailed information here allows us to gain an informed view of the varying circumstances surrounding sexual harassment in the church, particularly focusing on the unique power dynamics that are present when clergywomen experience it. At the same time that sexual harassment of clergywomen directs our focus to the politics of church institutions and community life, it is also intensely personal.

Whether it takes the form of a leering facial expression, jeering tone of voice, a sexually suggestive email, or an unwanted touch, sexual harassment invades the psyche of the person who is victimized. Workplace harassment is one of the most likely settings in which women experience male perpetrated sexual harassment. By the nature of their vocation clergywomen not only offer public leadership in front of congregations and other groups but also routinely provide personal attention to individuals within highly intimate settings where someone is ill, grief-stricken, suicidal, or in some other way spiritually and emotionally needy. The obligations of their Christian calling to serve needy people require spiritual and emotional outreach and vulnerability from clergywomen, which unfortunately can dovetail with the dynamics of sexual harassment.

For women who are harassed by male perpetrators, sexual harassment can produce a sense of bodily vulnerability that carries the threat of rape. In the aftermath of harassment a woman may feel insecure and self-conscious about how her body moves or how she dresses. The harasser's attempt to manipulate her often counts on shaming her into silence over just "a little joke" or "little pat". She may ask herself: "Will it shame my Latino/a community if I complain about this?" "Will anyone in my predominantly white community believe me since these things aren't supposed to happen to 'nice' white women like me?" Or, her silent embarrassment can fuel his enjoyment of the harassment. Multiple manipulative tactics by the perpetrator reinforce the lie that she has invited his attention (she reached out to him, didn't she?), that she has a problem, or she is the problem. His harassing behavior escapes culpability.

In the face of these dynamics, what is most important about Beth Cooper's study and our willingness to learn from it? It breaks the silence of institutional tolerance that harasser's count on to get away with their behavior. It reveals the problem as ours—those of us who participate in the church—to address. As the body of Christ, we must live out a theology that honors the fully embodied clergy leadership of women in the church with institutional practices that seek to prevent sexual harassment from occurring in the first place and have no tolerance for it when it does occur.

Introduction

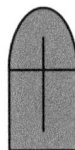

The Rev. Dr. Beth Cooper

The term "stained glass ceiling" refers to cultural and institutional limits placed on the ministry of clergywomen. Differentials between men and women in pay and promotions comprise part of the ceiling, but deeper examination reveals a range of life and cultural circumstances that make the situation complex. I chose the title *Under the Stained Glass Ceiling* to claim that sexual harassment of clergywomen stifles and limits the creativity and effectiveness of their ministries.

Today problems of gender and sexual harassment are widespread in churches. You may wonder why churches are not doing more to address these problems.

I saw a big problem around harassment of clergywomen and decided to pursue professional documentation. In 1997 I began interviewing clergywomen who had been harassed. I continued this project in a Women's Studies graduate certificate program and the results were shocking. So many women had experienced harassment and violence at the hands of parishioners and had nowhere to turn for help. I conducted the 2003 Survey of Clergywomen and Sexual Harassment in The United Methodist Church, the first study of its kind.[1] I received help and guidance from San Diego State University, especially from Dr. Kathleen Jones along with Dr. Susan Cayleff, Dr. Doreen Mattingly, and Dr. Barbara Watson of the Department of Women's Studies, the Human Subjects Research Committee and the Social Science Research Laboratory. The database was provided by

---

[1] Beth A. Cooper, *Do No Harm: Sexual Harassment against UM Clergywomen by Laity*, DMin. Dissertation, Wesley Theological Seminary, 2007.

the Commission on the Status and Role of Women (COSROW). The survey results published here are from the women clergy responses provided in 2003. The United Methodist Church, through COSROW, went on to conduct its own 2005 survey which confirmed the first study.[2] My research was detailed in two significant ways. I explored specific forms of harassment and also spoke with many clergywomen one on one, taking the time to hear their stories. I don't know whether others have taken the time to conduct formal interviews with hundreds of clergywomen.

In the time between when my research was conducted and the publication of this work, I fully expected that other studies would validate my research and build on the foundational work and that the public would learn of these problems from other reliable sources. The COSROW study confirmed this research, its validity and reliability, but the church did not stem the tide of problems faced by clergywomen.

Virtually nothing changed for clergywomen who continued to face the same problems. Clergywomen longed for a safe place to tell their stories in the hope that people would come to the aid of clergywomen. I continued interviewing and writing at Wesley Theological Seminary through a Doctor of Ministry program. The result was a dissertation and the seed for this book. I took my concerns to the 2008 General Conference of The United Methodist Church with petitions, supporters, and a small lobby. Although four petitions were adopted, others were not, and implementation has languished. In 2010 the Anna Howard Shaw Center at Boston University School of Theology conducted a survey on retention of clergywomen, a related field of study that has documented the continuing exodus of clergywomen from the profession of ministry.[3]

---

[2] The results of the COSROW study are available at www.gcrsw.org in the web archives.
[3] Anna Howard Shaw Center, "2010 Study of Retention of United Methodist Clergywomen," Boston University School of Theology, Boston, MA. This study has not been released as of the publication of this book.

Again there was no place to turn when I asked the church for help in publishing this book. Many saw sexual harassment of clergywomen as a problem with huge implications for changing the way the churches function.

How can we make churches safe places for women leaders? It won't be easy, but we can start by telling the truth.

Although time has passed since my initial research, the church and the public still has not heard the stories and the truth behind them. Now it is time.

More research is needed. We need to replicate the survey and find out whether women's experiences have changed. Are they the same, or are they better or worse? This book is an invitation to people who care and groups with deeper pockets to follow up with sound documentation to prove and reverse what appears to be true: Harassment of clergywomen takes place in every denomination with clergywomen. This is an invitation to churches and agencies whose reputations are at risk to clean up a mess and prevent additional harm. Clergywomen respond to God's call to service, yet this part of the body of Jesus Christ is still suffering. That is a call to action for all of us.

The book is structured to introduce the reader to the problem of sexual harassment of clergywomen and provide stories and illustrations that clarify the theme and its complexities. After raising awareness about how sexual harassment is widely experienced by clergywomen, various chapters describe contributing factors from law, culture, family systems, and assumptions that bolster practices of gender-based harassment. Only then does the book share specific survey statistics that substantiate claims of sexual harassment of clergywomen. The book explores directions for change and solutions available to the church, its leaders and members.

In the Preface, The Rev. Dr. Traci C. West ties biblical and theological teachings about God, sex/gender and power to cultural behaviors and assumptions that have failed to take seriously the problem of sexual harassment. "Femaleness" has been the object of ridicule, belittling, and abuse for thousands of years. The problem is ours and we must address it.

Chapter 1 opens the theme of the widespread occurrence of gender harassment and abuse of clergywomen and the power dynamics that lie behind misconduct. The chapter summarizes key research findings and asks about sexual harassment, "Is It Part of the Call?"

Chapter 2, "Clergywomen's Stories Remind Us of Our Truths," reveals the broad pervasive experience of the problem. From candidacy for ministry to retirement, from marital status to weight, from pregnancy to clothing choices, women are subjected to shame, embarrassment, humiliation and harassment.

Chapter 3, "Clergywomen and Family Systems," draws parallels between the ways families function and the relationship dynamics that operate within local churches. Gender and power issues at work in congregations influence predators and outcomes of sexual harassment. In the local church family systems may impede intervention and change. Stories from clergywomen and local churches expand our awareness of the scope of the problem.

Chapter 4, "Understanding Sexual Harassment," sets the problem of sexual harassment in historical context, providing an update on legal approaches to sexual harassment and an overview of civil and church law. Although The United Methodist Church has adopted official statements opposing sexual harassment and developed processes for bringing charges against lay persons, the problems persist.

"Can the church hold perpetrators accountable?" This question, posed in Chapter 5, traces various forms of legal recourse showing their ineffectiveness and the resulting lack of justice and protection for clergywomen. The call to ministry for women has not been accompanied with a commitment by the church to protect clergywomen from gender and sexual harassment.

Chapter 6, "The Crisis Revealed by Clergywomen," documents that sexual harassment of clergywomen is widespread. Harassment is perpetrated by persons of different races and geographical locations across the U.S. This chapter explores the political and social climate behind the incidents of sexual harassment, revealing the scope of the problem and the danger that it poses to the church and the gospel message.

Chapter 7, "Interpreting Clergywomen's Experiences," shares what this important survey of clergywomen shows, that clergywomen are a target for demeaning treatment by lay persons. They are not safe or being adequately protected.

Chapter 8, "Sexual Harassment and Leadership Issues," explores gender issues embedded in American culture and in the leadership of The United Methodist Church. There are systemic gender issues and leadership styles that produce dysfunctional outcomes. Breaking the silence around sexual harassment of clergywomen is an imperative step to effecting change.

In Chapter 9, tracing history from Anna Oliver, Sally Thompson and Anna Howard Shaw in the 1880s to the present, "The Long Tradition," documents the loss of clergywomen and how the church accepts departure of women who have been harassed or abused in lieu of addressing the core problems that cause this loss of leaders.

Chapter 10, "Do No Harm: A Principle for Redirection," calls The United Methodist Church to remember the general rule, "Do no harm," that John Wesley used to coach lay persons in Christian discipleship. Currently there has been little effort to teach church members to do no harm. If the denomination were to teach this simple, profound rule of Christian living and its implications to all church members, this could make a big difference.

Chapter 11, "Cultural Participation in Sexual Harassment," explores patterns, cultural assumptions and relationships that have made it difficult for the church to stop sexual harassment of clergywomen. Awareness of complex relationships in congregations is a vital key to making effective changes.

Chapter 12, "The Search for Solutions," considers ways that seminaries, annual conferences, local churches, general agencies, and connectional ministries can be part of a big cooperative effort to change the church's care for clergywomen and congregational health.

Chapter 13, "A Call to Action," offers specific suggestions for approaches that may be taken by annual conferences, local congregations, and clergywomen.

In Chapter 14, "Epilogue," Bishop Sally Dyck of the Minnesota Area of The United Methodist Church, offers analysis, meaning and implications of all these findings for congregations. She illustrates the power of taking action and challenges us to be the light shining through the stained glass windows of the church. She asks, "Whose face and eyes do the world see?"

The book's appendices supply materials designed for use by churches and church agencies. The covenant can be used in worship. Gender and sexual harassment policies for adults and children provide guidance. These resources may be copied, distributed and used by congregations and agencies for education and training purposes.

Is It Part of the Call?

When I answered the call to ministry, no one ever pulled me aside and explained to me that in the profession of ministry that I was entering at least half of clergywomen experience sexual harassment at the hands of laity.[4] This widespread problem, well documented over the past fifteen years, is hard to address because its proportions are so epidemic and cloaked. Ignorance, shame and culturally accepted gender inequities stand behind the problems that persist in the church. Our intent is to find answers and help for clergywomen so that all of us can help the church.

Culture, gender dynamics, social policies, and laws in the United States do not provide gender equality. The culture encourages gender inequities that are a primary basis for harassment and abuse. Clergywomen are a target for disrespect manifested in emotional, physical and sexual abuse. Our civil and church cultures still permit clergywomen to be treated in demeaning ways. This is part of a larger pattern.

In 1983, Marie Fortune began to study the impact of sexual abuse in the church. She published *Sexual Violence, the Unmentionable Sin*, a groundbreaking exposé and analysis which helped churches become aware of the abuse of women by clergymen.[5] People were stunned to see the breadth and scope of problems that had been masked for years.

---

[4] Beth A. Cooper, *Do No Harm: Sexual Harassment by Laity of United Methodist Clergywomen*, DMin. Dissertation, Wesley Theological Seminary, Washington, D.C., 2007.

[5] Marie Marshall Fortune, *Sexual Violence, The Unmentionable Sin: An Ethical and Pastoral Perspective*, New York: The Pilgrim Press, 1983.

We have come a long way. Church leaders and the general public know about sexual abuses. Church leaders have changed church policies, defined what is ethical and appropriate between clergy and laity, and implemented procedures designed to protect laity.

This study of clergywomen builds on the foundation laid by Marie Fortune who studied sexually abusive clergy. However this book deals with another problem--that persons in congregations take advantage of and abuse clergywomen. It focuses on sexual harassment of clergywomen, the dynamics at work in individuals, the church and the culture and makes recommendations for changes and new policies to help stem the tide of abuse.

The sexual harassment *of* clergywomen is different from sexual harassment *by* clergy. The two issues apply different dynamics which is why solving these problems requires different approaches.

The term "sexual harassment" has evolved since the 1970s. Sexual harassment can run the gamut from insensitive use of gestures or derogatory words to unwanted demands that demean and intimidate or coerce. Cultural values which contribute to objectification and degradation of women and girls do not magically stop at the doors of the church. Sexual harassment occurs in a context of power dynamics. This is the common theme of various approaches used to analyze the problem of the harassment of clergywomen that we now examine.

According to a 2005 survey taken by the General Commission of the Status Role of Women, three quarters of clergywomen and half of lay women have been sexually harassed in the local church.[6] The most commonly reported settings were church meetings, offices, and work places. United Methodist clergywomen are more likely to

---

[6] *Eradication of Sexual Harassment,*
http:www.gcsrw.org/EradicationofSexualHarassment.aspx. See also Gail Murphy-Geiss, "Sexual harassment in The United Methodist Church, 2005," (Chicago, Il: The General Commission on the Status and Role of Women, The United Methodist Church, 2005).

experience sexual harassment from laity than from their male colleagues.[7]

For thirty years The United Methodist Church has focused on the task of educating clergy for the prevention of clergy sexual harassment of laity. The church needs to be more aware of what happens when laity sexually harass clergy, particularly clergywomen. By focusing on clergy as perpetrators and lay persons as victims, scholars and church leaders initially missed a major problem. It is true that clergy have power by virtue of office. This can mean that male laity have power of gender and may harass clergywomen. In many situations, the dynamics of gender can trump the power of office.

Any combination is possible. Clergywomen may harass others. Lay women may harass lay men. However, it is far more likely that lay men will harass lay women. If lay men harass clergywomen, they also are likely to harass lay women. In desiring to deal with the complexities of the situation of clergywomen, this book focuses on harassment of clergywomen by laity as one aspect of a large spectrum of sexual misconduct.

In order to understand misconduct and provide effective intervention, it is crucial to ask who has power and how gender is perceived. Other differentials in power commonly known include race, economic position, age, host/guest, and experience. More power tends to accrue to persons with lighter skin, more money, age or experience, and to those providing hospitality.

The power of the office of clergy has changed. In earlier times, clergy stood in a place of respect and authority in the community. In part this was due to their education. As recently as thirty years ago, with seven years of college and graduate school, clergy were among the most educated members of the community. With more people earning college and graduate degrees, the ranks of highly educated people have swelled. The educational aspect of their office has less power than in the past. With the entry of significant numbers of

---

[7] Beth A. Cooper, "Do No Harm: Sexual Harassment against UM Clergywomen by Laity" (D. Min. Dissertation, Wesley Theological Seminary, 2007).

13

clergywomen, the feminization of the profession has been accompanied by "diminished authority."[8] While women may be holding more substantial leadership positions in the church, the culture has started to devalue the office of clergy. One causal factor behind this is that more women are in leadership. We have not dealt with the root of gender prejudice.

Respect for authority in the field of morality and ethics is now shared with mental health professionals, doctors and lawyers. Some clergy have dishonored their profession by engaging in sexual misconduct. Leaders in the field of religion command less authority than in the past.

The changes in times and status may leave clergy more vulnerable. It takes cultural awareness and the cooperation of everyone in a church taking seriously appropriate behavior in the area of sexual conduct to truly create a safe sanctuary. For a church to nurture people in spiritual growth, its sanctuaries must be safe. When incidents of gender or sexual harassment take place, too often leaders may make excuses.

Attitudes and expectations so permeate the culture, religious institutions and persons that predictable patterns emerge. Even with civilized people living in a democratic nation, why would ordinary people engage in unspeakable acts? Why would an ordinary church member harass or attack a clergywoman, in secret or in public, with intent to demean, intimidate or harm?

When the church teaches biblical stories showing that Jesus respected persons regardless of gender, women entering ministry may assume that women will be well received and not encounter subversion and resistance. Some of these women consider that the clergywomen who went before them brought problems on themselves by being pushy. They may imagine that by not being politically radical or liberal they will not have to face resistance. It may leave the fresh generation of clergywomen vulnerable and naïve

---

[8] Paula D. Nesbitt, *Feminization of the Clergy in America: Occupational and Organizational Perspectives* (New York, NY: Oxford University Press, 1997) 26.

14

if they think that they won't experience sexual harassment because this was a thing of the past.

Church policies need to be reviewed. Clergywoman can prepare to deal with sexual harassment by becoming familiar with secular and church laws, their interpretations and applications. Clergywomen may minimize problems by establishing protocols and procedures such as keeping meeting room doors open, recording sessions, referring people to professional counselors, and working with others present rather than one on one.

Sexual harassment, as with other forms of violence, takes many shapes. It varies from minor incidents to major life-changing events. Research has been conducted to discern responses to violence and to explore how violence becomes culturally acceptable. Large groups of people can be persuaded to accept the use of violence. Given the right conditions, cultural norms and a crowd mentality legitimize harassing speech, intimidating emotions, threatening behavior, and violent actions.

The research of John Conroy has explored the process that takes place and what happens to persuade a majority of people to agree that it is permissible, even beneficial, to tolerate or use violence. There is a common thread that shows up in these processes, whether the violence involved is elementary school bullying, harassment of clergywomen, or torture of political prisoners. Harassment, violence and torture may seem to be quite different and distinct, but close examination shows many similarities. It is valuable to understand the process that has enabled tolerance and acceptance of sexual harassment of clergywomen as a norm.

John Conroy conducted a study of the dynamics and practices of torture in nations where one might not expect to find it occurring.[9] The language and behaviors leap out as all too familiar and offer an interpretation that goes well beyond excusing perpetrators for isolated actions. The acquiescence of bystanders to events can enable

---

[9] John Conroy, *Unspeakable Acts, Ordinary People: The Dynamics of Torture* (Berkeley, CA: University of California Press, 2000).

outrageous behavior to be perpetuated. Meanwhile, sometimes those who know what is happening manipulate the message to defend unspeakable acts and inappropriate behavior. Harassment may thrive in a climate that readily defends these acts. If a society can embody prejudice and discrimination against women, so can the culture in the church.

According to Conroy, there are nine stages in the acceptance of violence. The stages are denying, minimizing, disparaging, justifying, accusing, labeling, blaming, comparing, and accepting. We apply these stages to what takes place in congregations.[10]

When an incident is reported, the first stage of response may be absolute and complete denial, accompanied by attacks on those who exposed the situation. In the church we hear denials such as, "[The perpetrator] wouldn't do that." "[The clergywoman] is looking for publicity and fame." "[Our clergywoman] just doesn't care about the church." "[This lay member] has given so much of his time for the church, he wouldn't be so hurtful."

The second stage is to minimize abuse which then is described as having no permanent effect. In a church setting people might minimize the abuse by saying such things as, "It was a harmless misunderstanding." "There was no lasting injury." "He was hard on her because he just wanted to show her how to do her best." "They were both participating in mutual intimacy."

The third stage is to disparage the victims and put them down. The ecclesiastical version of this might have a perpetrator saying to the victim, "Come on. You know you were asking for it." "Why do you have to be such a 'slut?'" "Are you trying to shame my family?" To add further insult to a clergywoman and to justify their harassment or abuse, church leaders and members might continue to put the victim down.

---

[10] John Conroy, Ibid., 31-40. In the following pages, Conroy's nine stages are listed. He made these observations about nations discrediting their incidents of torture.

The fourth stage justifies the treatment "on grounds that it is effective or an appropriate action under the circumstances."[11] In a church setting people might justify abuse of a clergywoman saying, "The Bible doesn't say anything about this." "She prostituted herself to get ahead." Church leaders might gather hearsay evidence, make judgments and conclude, "We have heard from others that there might be a pattern here."

The fifth stage claims that those who take up the cause of the victim are helping those who would harm the institution. In a church setting, opinion in the congregation may be split. Church members might criticize other church members who take up the cause of the clergywoman for taking sides with one who is sinning and going against God. Church members might say, "They are taking up a feminist cause that isn't biblical." "They are troublemakers, ineffective, and need to be cut out of the life of the church." Examples of action would be shunning, shaming, isolating, and bullying. Propaganda would be spread against the group.

In the sixth stage, people claim that the violence is no longer occurring and that anyone who raises the issue is "raking up the past." Church members might claim, "This clergywoman is a troublemaker who wants to destroy the church." "The church cannot move forward if this keeps getting thrown in our faces."

At the seventh stage, blame is put on a few people. The church may punish a perpetrator or two, prohibit them from holding leadership, and ask for a public apology.

The eighth stage asserts that someone else has done much worse things. Members of a congregation might participate in this stage by saying, "Why are we focusing on this?" "This is one isolated incident." "The church needs to concentrate on other things."

In the ninth stage, people claim that the victims will get over it.[12] Yet almost never does one get over such treatment. Harassment and trauma are not erased. A survivor may have to learn to live beyond

---

[11] Ibid., 35.
[12] John Conroy, 244-246.

the experience and integrate it into her life. Statements that outsiders make about "getting over it" carry little sensitivity or compassion about what actually has happened.

These stages are familiar.. When it comes to putting a stop to such behaviors, the larger the group involved, the slower it is to respond to change. Churches have done little to address problems of sexual harassment of clergywomen.

When I interviewed United Methodist clergywomen from across the U.S. on the subject of sexual harassment, certain patterns emerged that described their experience with sexual harassment. Here are some key findings.

1) Sexual harassment has no prejudice. Women have experienced sexual harassment regardless of age, class, race or marital status or region.

2) Despite policies on sexual harassment adopted and implemented in the church, over half of clergywomen who served in ministry have experiences of sexual harassment while on the job.

3) Clergywomen need support through education of church leaders and members of congregations in implementation of policies and procedures.

4) When perpetrators call clergywomen names such as lesbian, dyke, whore, and bitch, these "put down" terms do not refer to the clergywoman's sexual orientation or sexuality but are assaults on the clergywoman's character to which perpetrators feel entitled due to her gender.

5) The most frequent incidents of sexual harassment of clergywomen are attributed to laity. Occurring less frequently are incidents by other clergy and church leaders. However, sexual harassment incidents perpetrated by clergy colleagues will occur when clergy can get away with being more covert.

Sexual harassment takes place in every state and nation among people of every race and culture. Even the most intentional and careful clergywomen can be victims. Responsible communities of faith do not want to be a place where violence is committed and people are not safe. Our part is to learn more about the problem and answer the call to action.

Clergywomen Remind Us of the Truth

2

Stories from clergywomen serving the United Methodist Church and women affiliated with The United Methodist Church who felt called to ministry reveal the scope of the problem of sexual harassment of clergywomen. From the first steps that women take in exploring ordination to the end of a clergy career, clergywomen have encountered sexual harassment. Frequently their experiences with gender harassment were a pivotal point in their decision about what happened next. These stories show the widespread nature of abuse within the church and how challenging it is to overcome sexism.

Starting the Process and Exploring Candidacy

At every turn in the process of ministry, gender issues and sexism play a significant role for women in ministry. Often these weigh in with greater influence than that which comes with ministerial office or an official position within the church.

I interviewed a woman who had completed her seminary training because she wanted to be in mission through the church. She had been an exploring candidate for ministry, but at the time I met her she had changed her mind and had no intention of finishing the candidacy program to become a clergy person.

Before the days of digital communication she was in college and felt a call to ministry. She started to explore leadership programs within the church. She did quite well. She held different positions in her church, district, and annual conference. She decided to participate in a mission program within The United Methodist Church. She trusted the system. When she was sent overseas, she discovered that her field supervisor was not living in town. She had no one to whom she could go for parental or adult guidance and support.

She was in a country where the sentiment was anti-U.S. at the time. She felt unsafe. She and her female teammate were assigned to a living situation that was not safe for women. The neighborhood had problems and the door lacked adequate security. One night, shortly after she arrived, she and her teammate were attacked in their room while sleeping. The woman that I interviewed had been gang raped. It was weeks before they received help from the mission program.

Years later, while sharing her experience and about how the church failed her, she realized that even though she had been pressed to the edge and back, God was calling her to ministry. She couldn't understand. How could one serve an institution that does not protect its young or its women? Why would an institution care more for its system than its people? She didn't rule out God's call, but because of her experience, she still had to work through deep emotional issues.

Another woman entered her candidacy program and was assigned to work with a faculty member of the seminary where she was enrolled. The man supervising her candidacy was both a teacher and ordained in The United Methodist Church. At first things seemed fine. She would meet with her supervisor and they would go over the manual, discuss related questions that grew out of the program, and process her questions about the church and ministry.

As weeks went by, she became uneasy and fearful of her supervisor. He wanted her to meet him at his office. He started to act too familiar and asked inappropriate questions, such as if she were married, or dating, and other questions about her sexual experience. The student left his office and went to the Dean of Students who was a good friend of the faculty member. The Dean said that the faculty member would be reprimanded, but the student remembered wondering, "Where could I go and who would believe me?"

A very successful clergywoman recalled doing her church internship to fulfill field education requirements for seminary and her annual conference. One day while she was in her office the senior pastor entered and came on to her. She was stunned by his actions. She spent weeks trying to dodge him. She wondered where she could go to report his behavior.

When she finally went to the district superintendent she was told that it would be her word against the senior pastor, and that the incident would follow her while she was being considered for ministry. To this day she remembers the hurt she felt. She did nothing wrong but became trapped in a system that did not provide support when she needed it.

Separation of church and state enables churches to avoid protecting the civil rights of clergywomen. Church committees take liberties that are not permitted in the workplace. Women have been asked peculiar questions that, if asked in any other setting, by law would be a violation of privacy and an act of discrimination. Women who are entering ministry encounter sexism, sexual harassment, and abuse.

A second career woman sought ordination in her annual conference. Recently divorced, the details of the divorce were not the business of the interview. The interviewing committee asked her if her desire to pursue ordained ministry was the reason behind her divorce.

One woman who was overweight remembered how embarrassed she was when her District Committee on Ordained Ministry commented on her weight and suggested that this might keep her from being ordained. When they asked her if she thought she was overweight due to a medical issue, she looked directly at two overweight men in the room and stated that she wished that were the case and that she noticed that countless men serving in the conference were overweight.

Issues around marital status and weight

Marital status and weight can be used inappropriately against women. If a woman were in any other occupation, even if it were difficult for her to provide evidence proving sexual harassment, the law provides an avenue for redress of grievances, even if it might mean going to the American Civil Liberties Union (ACLU) to seek protection for liberties. Unfortunately, the ACLU can't help clergywomen. Recourse for advocacy is not available in the church.

A woman who was part of a clergy couple found it hard when her husband was sent to serve an appointment on the opposite side of the conference. The district superintendent tried to find another local church near her husband's assignment. He asked her to serve this appointment but did not give the congregation any preparation or training to receive their first clergywoman. The district superintendent did not provide an opportunity for members of the congregation to discuss their fears or express their anger for being assigned a clergywoman. When they were told they were getting a clergywoman, the congregation panicked. They sent the news all over the small town. Just when the clergywoman believed that she was winning people over, violence broke out. Someone shot at her. On three different occasions someone shot at her.

The district superintendent vowed to a hold a laity trial but experienced utter chaos with his responsibilities to the church and to the community, in addition to his obligations to the clergywoman. He couldn't pull it together to pursue the investigation and requirements of a trial. Eventually the clergywoman was moved, but the appointive cabinet blamed her for forcing the denomination to move her husband as well.

I interviewed several clergy couples where the women and men served the same appointment but the pay check was given to the man. In some cases the husband was given the full time appointment while the wife was assigned quarter time or half time. There also were cases were women served with their husbands but a pension was paid for the husband and not the wife.

Single clergywomen face difficulties as well. A single, young clergywoman was appointed to a church three hours away from any major city. She lived and worked in a smaller town where everyone knew everyone else and most of the people were related to each other. Private opportunities for recreation or play or have a personal life with friends outside the community was nearly impossible. She lived in a fish bowl. Yet, when the clergywoman tried to take her day off and go to the city, members of the congregation would ask questions as if she were a teenager in their family. "Where did you go?" "Who were you with?" "Why did you get back so late?" If she began answering their inappropriate questions, she wondered where it would end.

By not completely answering the questions, she paid a price. Church people felt that if she didn't answer the questions she must be hiding something. If she came home late, she must be with someone.

Single clergywomen that I interviewed frequently said that it was hard to have a life outside the church because of social presumptions. They explained that no friendship is safe from presumptions. If you are seen with a man, you must be "loose." If you are seen with a woman, you must be a lesbian.

In one congregation, members told a divorced clergywoman that they didn't know if the appointment would work because it was obvious that she was a failure. If she couldn't hold her marriage together, how would she ever be successful at their church? They gave no credence to relationships being a combination of factors.

Perhaps the most vulnerable status for clergywomen is that of being divorced or widowed with children. The single parent female pastor has the added responsibility of protecting her children. One clergywoman who moved to an extension ministry from the local church said that she was tired of the church using her children to get personal information about her instead of asking her directly.

Appropriate Dress

In her book, *Sexual Shame*, Karen McClintock describes one congregation where she was asked to wear a robe in worship. Women's fashions at the time called for skirts or dresses to be worn to church. Some parishioners were uncomfortable seeing her knees, especially in the sanctuary. This situation that generated shame for McClintock began when members of the congregation objectified her. They had a problem dealing with their own sexual feelings. After this incident and for twenty five years, McClintock never led worship without a robe because of the sexual shame she felt.[13]

The situation could have been nipped in the bud if the senior pastor or members of the congregation had stepped forward and asserted her right to wear women's clothing appropriate to the day. They could have set a standard that did not teach sexual shame. The insidious side of these seemingly minor incidents is that they put down women and inhibit a woman's ability to rise to her full potential.

One woman told me that she didn't like to wear make-up. She was aware of how many billions of dollars go to corporations that send the message that women are nothing without make-up. To her, it was a part of her ministry and call to justice to look nice and neat but to not wear anything that would promote the idea that a woman did not have natural beauty. She was told by her Staff Parish Relations Committee (SPRC) that she needed to start wearing make up because she was a professional. By not wearing make-up, they said, she was modeling a role that was not appropriate.

Not long after this I interviewed another clergywoman who loved to wear make-up. She enjoyed getting manicures and pedicures. She regularly went out to get her hair done and occasionally would take spa days as her way to pamper herself. When she let other people work on her it reminded her how precious and beautiful she was. She was called into her staff parish relations committee because members

---

[13] Karen McClintock, *Sexual Shame, An Urgent Call to Healing* (Minneapolis: Augsburg Fortress Press, 2001), 1-3.

felt that she was not being professional. One person on the committee told her that she looked like a "slut" and wore too much red lipstick. Other people could not believe that she would spend her money on such things so frivolous when there were so many mission needs. She told me, "I could not believe how these people felt. Not only did they presume to tell me what I could and could not do at work, but also how I was to spend my money, and what I was to look like at work."

Violence in the Workplace

A clergywoman recounted a terrible experience that took place while she was working in the church. She had put in a long day and was getting ready to leave. She remembered hearing sounds in the church but thought it was the wind. When she went to turn her office lights out and walk out to the hallway, she was attacked from behind. She never saw her attacker's face. Her perpetrator sodomized her and raped her for hours. When he finally left, she had bruises on most of her body and she was bleeding from her vagina and rectum.

She told someone in her family who was also a United Methodist church member. The family member, outraged, called the district superintendent. The district superintendent paid a visit to the clergywoman who was grieving and angry. She couldn't focus and was not able to sleep through the night on account of what had happened. The district superintendent did not advise the woman to go to the police. The superintendent did not mention that the church was supportive of her or cared about her or her health. Instead the superintendent said, "Why don't you take two of your vacation weeks and go away and try to get this behind you?"

I interviewed her eight years after this horrific event in her life. When I asked her what happened after she came back she said, "I went away for two weeks and came back and preached as if nothing happened. I did my job, finished out the year, and asked for a leave. I never, nor do I ever, care to serve a local church again."

A woman considering ordination held a position on one of the committees at General Conference. Her office required her to be on stage for the presentation of the committee report. While she was on stage a group of people interrupted the program with an act of civil disobedience on the floor of the General Conference. She decided to stand in solidarity with those who were protesting.

The chair of her committee reached over, grabbed her arm, and pulled her down. His physical strength bruised her arm. She was shocked and stunned with embarrassment that, in public or any time, a man would presume to decide her stance on any issue. Another man forced him to release his grip on her, but to this day, she cannot get over the arrogance of the one who presumed that he had the right to control her.

A clergywoman told about a time she was being stalked. A church member had asked her to run an errand on his behalf. He wasn't a person who could handle being told "No." When the clergywoman said no, the man got very upset. He threatened her, saying that she would live to regret her decision. After that the man started to show up at inappropriate times at the parsonage and follow her from place to place. This continued for weeks. When she went to the police, the police said that stalking was hard to prove and that a crime had not yet been committed. She needed to be on guard and call them when he made his move. The clergywoman finished the year and moved to another appointment.

It doesn't take physical violence for a clergywoman to know that her appointment is not a safe place. One clergywoman told me that she had been experiencing problems with her appointment to her church. One Friday she decided to meet some friends for dinner. After all, it was her day off.

She drove out of town for about two hours to meet friends. She stopped only one time along the way to use the bathroom. She kept feeling that she was being followed. She looked around and didn't see anything out of the ordinary. Her feeling was strong but she thought that maybe the appointment was getting the best of her and making her paranoid. She arrived at the restaurant located in a nice hotel. The restaurant was known throughout the area for its excellent food. She waited on her friends for about twenty minutes, and while she was waiting, decided to call her district superintendent because she could not shake the feelings that she was having. She dialed and explained why she was calling. She said that it was probably nothing but wanted him to know that it was her day off and she decided to drive to see some special friends and have a meal with them.

The district superintendent asked her a question that changed her life. "If you are having a meal with friends then why are you parked outside a hotel?" She had not mentioned anything about a hotel, but the district superintendent knew exactly where she was.

At that moment she knew she was not safe. It was apparent that not only was someone following her but that they followed her for a significant amount of time, and that they wanted to do damage because in such a short time they had already called the district superintendent. Not only was a woman stalked, but the district superintendent was entertaining gossip and hearsay without putting the stalker on alert for being inappropriate. When church leaders participate, even by doing nothing, they extend the damages and harm of sexism.

Because of repeated incidents such as these, many clergywomen spoke of not feeling safe in their work environment. Violence escalates when boundaries are not honored or enforced. Just as lynching was used in the past by white men to keep African Americans submissive, in our culture today, men use violence or the fear of violence to keep women in their place. Rape is a part of that control and violence. While most men don't rape, each such crime that occurs reminds all women of the heightened threat that men hold over them. It is insidious because violence can happen almost anytime, anywhere—in public buildings, on streets, when women are at home, and when women are at church. Some movies still depict men controlling women through threat and violence, reflecting a negative social value that lives on alive and well in our culture. Men may do harm to maintain control over women. Rape and murder are ultimate crimes repeated daily.

Clergywomen are no safer than other women in the work place. In part, their lack of safety has been attributed to crossing a gender boundary by entering what has traditionally been a men's profession. Theological and scriptural arguments have been used to fortify cultural practices such as excluding women from the clergy. People came to believe what religious authorities told them, without being aware of the cultural contexts of these practices. People who have not discovered the cultural limitations of these teachings may defend them with physical, emotional and abusive power. Wilbur Bick has pointed out:

> Women are not completely accepted by the public or by their male colleagues in their professional roles....however the degree of marginality of women varies among different professions. One profession that apparently is quite, if not most, resistant to change is the clergy, which has been defined as masculine but as "sacredly" masculine.[14]

Stages of Womanhood

A younger clergywoman talked about the pain of her first appointment. Her mother, father, and brother had died in an automobile accident while she was away at college. She entered her first appointment where the church did not want a woman pastor, let alone a single, young clergywoman. As she started her first year she was met with all kinds of ridicule and resistance. Finally, in the heat of the moment, the head of trustees said to her, "It must be very painful for you to do a job that no one thinks you should be doing. Even your family doesn't feel that you should be doing it." When the clergywoman asked why he would say that about her family, she was told that it was obvious because her family never came to visit her,

---

[14] E. Wilbur Bick, "Female Clergy: A Case of Professional Marginality" *The American Journal of Sociology*, 72:5 (March 1967), University of Chicago Press, 531-539.

came to any worship services, or gatherings at the church. The church never reached out beyond their bias to know this young woman who was serving their church.

Another clergywoman talked about how she was having a very difficult pregnancy. Although she had carried other pregnancies to term, this baby was bigger than any of the others. At times she found it difficult to care for her self during the pregnancy, but she always loved doing church work. Although she had other children, this was her first pregnancy while serving this church. She was called into the staff parish relations committee meeting so that they could tell her that she needed to wear an oversized robe because several of the men had commented that her clothing was too tight. It made them uncomfortable in worship. She started wearing her robe, but anyone could tell that she was pregnant because of her belly. Again she was called into the staff parish relations committee because, yet again, people were reminded that she was pregnant.

This situation hints at differences in the ways people are perceived according to gender. Men do not have any visual consequences for having sex. When people see a pregnant woman, they know she had sex. This alone can prompt people to think about sex. The thoughts run through their heads. Then church leaders ask pregnant women to take care of this problem.

There's something wrong with this picture. The church adds a layer of shame by expecting that a clergywoman should not represent the reality of sexuality, even with such a normal part of life as bearing a child. This is not a problem for clergymen.

Clergywomen don't have to be pregnant to receive sexual comments. Some members of the congregation, especially men, are uncomfortable because they see a woman who elicits sexual desire. A man may not only fear his own response. He may be uncomfortable simply because he sees a woman and knows the potential of having a sexual response. Even in these times when many people promote gender equality, some people equate women with sexuality and respond by making them sexual objects or objects of sexual pursuit.

For clergywomen who never climbed the corporate ladder and who draw closer to retirement, gender issues are present. Many clergywomen have run into the stained glass ceiling effect, the unspoken cap that limits their ministries. Some of these clergywomen talked with me about how men who were ordained at the same time that they were now earned substantially larger incomes. These larger salaries pay larger pensions in retirement, so the difference has long term consequences.

The New York Times looked into this matter and published an article on clergywomen and how they are being paid less than their male counterparts. The article noted that "In their second decade in ordained ministry, however, 70 percent of men had moved on to medium-sized and large congregations.... By comparison, only 37 percent of women led medium and large larger congregations."[15]

Clergywomen of color experience a doubly adverse effect. Bishop Leontine Kelly often repeated that one of the things that saddened her was that the church would never know the full potential of its clergy of color and its clergywomen because of the amount of energy it took just to deal with the walls of racism and sexism. The obstacles waste energy that could be applied creatively to implement the vision and move the church forward.[16]

I wish that I could have recorded and shared all of the stories of clergywomen that I interviewed over ten years. This was not possible because there are situations that are too specific that would be too damaging to individuals and congregations. Many clergywomen are still in situations where they might experience repercussions and personal harm for telling what has happened to them. Even though each story has value and is precious, sadly there are so many common

---

[15] *New York Times,* August 26, 2006, 11.

[16] Leontine Kelly, A presentation to the Holy Boldness Convocation, an Urban Ministries Conference of The United Methodist Church, San Francisco, Nov.22-25, 1997. Bishop Kelly used this theme in numerous speeches in various locations including Perkins School of Theology, Western Pennsylvania Conference, and various clergywomen's conferences. Bishop Kelly shared stories illustrating how the church participates in "isms." Kelly focused on what the church is and could be.

points and repeated occurrences that sometimes the stories repeat while only the names and places change. This is a painful picture.

During the time in which I conducted these interviews I was fortunate to be a part of many different women's circles where women shared their pain and joys at being called by God to ministry and simultaneously having to live out their calling in an imperfect world full of fear and hate. I heard stories and continued to receive phone calls from clergywomen of different cultures and races, marital status, age, and areas of the United States.

Clergywomen who have been hurt or do not trust the United Methodist system want to talk in a safe setting. They want someone to know their truth that some church people are cruel. Cruel behavior conflicts with Jesus' admonition to love one another and to the church's rule and guide to do no harm.

Clergywomen and Family Systems 3

An introduction to family systems study and to both civil and church law helps lay a foundation for understanding sexual and gender harassment in the church. The meaning of boundaries is crucial to lay empowerment, leadership, and training for lay pastors and the mission of the church.

A church system operates with remarkable similarity to a family system. This can be harmful when the family system handles church business and conflict in dysfunctional and unhealthy ways.

Power dynamics in local churches have been analyzed by applying family systems theory to demonstrate power dynamics at work in the church. As in a family in which members have roles and carry out functions, members of congregations have roles and functions, status and position, with power dynamics at work. Church members live in relation to each other very much as they would within a family.

Candace R. Benvei's book, *Understanding Clergy Misconduct in Religious Systems,* discusses the relationship between behavior, power, and history. The author points to the additional factor of the history of patterns that exist in congregations.

> The religious community is not a gathering of separate persons, but an interrelated system.... All the rules of a community are an evolutionary product of its history. The behavior of persons in the community is also determined by where they are placed in relation to others in the congregational structure. This has to do with issues of power...[17]

---

[17] Candace R. Banyei, *Understanding Clergy Misconduct in Religious Systems: Scapegoating, Family Secrets, and the Abuse of Power,* (New York: Haworth Pastoral Press, 1998), 1-2.

Especially if family members fear that the family system is threatened, changing, or falling apart, they are likely to support unhealthy behaviors within the family system. For this reason, a family system may harbor shame or a secret. A family may cover up problems or protect and defend members who abuse power.

No family system is stagnant. When changes occur, family members adapt their roles to those around them. Some family members have greater power and others less or virtually none. Some have voice in deliberations and others are dismissed. These changes take place in congregations as well.

The impact of a family system in a congregation becomes transparent when people hold office for a long time. Persons in power grow accustomed to their habits of leadership and become entrenched in their style. The long tenure stunts growth and gives the person in office a false sense of ownership. Sometimes, instead of emphasizing life lived in response to God, the emphasis begins to focus on the individual.

A certain man served as the church's chair of trustees for over thirty years. He had keys to the church and to every room, including the pastor's office and parsonage. He announced far and wide that he never wanted a clergywoman for his pastor. When a clergywoman arrived, he began to use his keys inappropriately, entering the parsonage unannounced, uninvited and in her absence. He used the privilege of his gender and office to intimidate and create a hostile environment for the clergywoman both at work and at home. Members of the church knew his behavior was wrong, but wouldn't stop him. They were afraid of his bullying and couldn't conceive of anyone else in the role of chairperson of the trustees, because, after all, he had held this office for such a long time. This created a perfect setup for harassment on the basis of gender.

Issues of domestic violence often are part of a church family system and their presence is closely related to sexual harassment. Just as women stay in battering relationships for many reasons including economic dependence, isolation, shame, fear and perceptions of biblical teachings, these same issues are at work for clergywomen who experience sexual harassment and stay in a battering relationship in the church.

One clergywoman that I interviewed spoke about the hurt she felt when she was sexually harassed by a lay person in the church she was serving. She had participated in meals and events with him and his family. She had been pastor to the family when one of the children had been in accident and died. Regularly they prayed and worshipped together. She spoke of sharing smiles and tears in meaningful times. The joy of this relationship was shattered because, after the man tried to touch her inappropriately, she was afraid to be in the same room with him. She grieved this loss. She felt that because of her place of employment and how she viewed her relationship with the church that, indeed, sexual harassment felt like domestic violence occurring in the church.

Every congregation has leaders who set expectations and standards for the congregation, but sometimes leaders are very controlling. They may dominate others or control what happens in a church. Their power may continue until their death or until an untimely trauma occurs in the church or community. Sometimes the power of strong laity has the ability to trump the power of clergy. Clergywomen experience this more often than male clergy. In local church politics, clergy have power in places of counseling. Clergy may be strong preachers, teachers and administrators, but their power reaches limits when controlling church leaders oppose them. Engaging in dialogue about how church members have power in different settings provides a service that can be helpful to correcting problems of sexual misconduct.

When a pastor begins his or her work in a new congregation, there may be a period of initiation and testing, a honeymoon period, of six months to a year. The pastor and congregation make assess each other to see whether the match is going to make it or not. If not, members of the congregation may begin to take steps to make life very uncomfortable for the new pastor.

Church members made life miserable and ministry impossible for a clergywoman assigned to a congregation in the Northeast. The congregation decided before she arrived that they did not want to accept her leadership. The clergywoman, a single mother with three children, was sent to a church where the parsonage was uninhabitable. Her district superintendent (DS) told her to give the congregation time because he was sure that eventually they would warm up to her, do the right thing, repair and maintain the parsonage. After several months of living in a place that was inappropriate for children, and being warned not to rock the boat, she felt distressed because nothing was moving forward. She would attend meetings and be ignored. At one frustrating meeting the trustees acted as though she wasn't present.

Because of this, she decided to make a list itemizing parsonage repairs and maintenance that were overdue. The clergywoman gave the list to the chair of the trustees. The list indicated what was needed urgently, what could wait a couple of months, and which items were long term issues. She was surprised that the head of the trustees took the list.

Several weeks later she learned that she was being investigated by Children's Services for neglecting to provide a safe and appropriate place for her children to live. The chair of the trustees had taken her handwritten list to Adult and Family Services and filed a complaint that his pastor was not being an appropriate mother.

After she was investigated, the charges were dropped. Adult and Family Services found her more than qualified to raise her children.

Consider the damages. Because of the charges and investigation, an incredible amount of distrust was spread around the community. Because this took place in a small town, the damage from gossip was terrible. The pastor said:

> They might as well have painted a red letter on my chest. The amount of stress and conflict management that I had to deal with zapped my energy from doing real visionary work with

the church and took away what quality time that I could have had with my children.

More importantly, I felt that the church leadership really let me down. The DS knew how resistant this church was to woman leadership but she neglected to see "how far they would go." In the end, when they did get inappropriate, the church and the church leadership did nothing. Although, I did nothing wrong, it was no fun and actually quite harmful what all my family and I endured. After reflecting on my experience, not only am I convinced that this could have been handled differently but I don't believe that God called me to do ministry in that type of setting.[18]

Five years after these experiences, although she had been through healing and was working through her trauma issues, it was evident that this event had changed her life.

One clergywoman repeatedly was sexually harassed the day before she received her paycheck that was given to her by the perpetrator. She told me that she felt like a "prostitute for Christ."[19] Was she being paid for his pleasure?

On another occasion I interviewed a single young clergywoman from the Midwest who was struggling to decide whether to stay in the local church or move into a specialized ministry.[20] She had served as an associate pastor and then was sent to another local church. When I met her, she was taking a year of Clinical Pastoral Education to work through some things that she wanted to examine in her ministry. Her experiences in the parish had traumatized her.

The patriarch of the church asked if she would come to his house to go over some business. She remembers thinking that this would be appropriate because everyone looked up to him and he did so much

[18] Anonymous, interview 3 by author, 12 January, 2002, San Diego, CA, interview in person, notes.
[19] Anonymous, interview 41 by author, 12 September, 2002, San Diego, CA, interview in person, notes.
[20] Anonymous, interview 79 by author, 10 March, 2003, San Diego, CA, interview by telephone, notes.

for the church. He was tall and easy going. Not once did she pick up any red flag warnings about him or his character. When she arrived at his home, he asked her to come in and have prayer with him. When she started to pray she noticed that he had positioned himself so that his body was touching hers. He grabbed her hand and told her to do sexual acts for him. When she said that she wouldn't, he said that he would tell the church that she came on to him and say, "You see, you can't trust a woman minister." She felt that because the truth was on her side, she had nothing to fear.

In fact, she had much to fear. She described her next eight months as total hell. Because the church knew the man for countless years, they chose his story over the pastor's. What was a lie had become this congregation's truth.

The community was embroiled in a sea of gossip. Gossip enlarged and expanded the one incident so that it grew into more incidents with more people. She began to feel that her life was threatened, and she packed up her things and left.

When gender-based trauma takes place, women may experience a string of multiple traumas that I call "two-tone incidents." The first trauma, difficult in its own right, triggers a follow-up sequence of traumatic events. The second part can be more harmful than the first when the community gossips and rallies around the perpetrator. When a perpetrator engages in numerous invasions of privacy and other forms of harassment, this heightens the amount of trauma and the work needed for recovery. Gossip and innuendos often are followed by silence or shunning. These, too, are forms of trauma.

No longer can we simply claim that the clergyperson always has power and the layperson does not. It is a travesty within the church not to examine these power dynamics. In an age when there is so much written about lay empowerment and lay leadership, the church also needs to teach appropriate behavior. Failure to deal with the power held by laity has contributed to countless acts of trauma against clergywomen. It is crucial to understand what behavior is appropriate and what is not.

Understanding Sexual Harassment 4

Legal definitions of sexual harassment have changed over time. For many years The United Methodist Church appropriated the 1980 definition of sexual harassment issued by The U.S. Equal Employment Opportunities Commission. Sexual harassment was defined as "unwelcome sexual advances, requests for sexual favors, and other verbal or physical conduct of a sexual nature" [21] when the conduct or its acceptance or rejection interferes with a person's work or becomes a condition of employment or creates an intimidating or offensive work environment.

To that early definition of sexual harassment were added other concepts developed in U.S. Supreme Court landmark decisions, including, in 1986, an understanding of "unwanted conduct" and in 1992, the interpretation that workers should not be demeaned, humiliated or intimidated on the basis of their gender. In 1998-99 in Davis v. Monroe, the Supreme Court added the notion that schools may be held liable for students' harassment of other students if officials knew about it and did nothing to stop it. Courts have held various jurisdictions of the Roman Catholic Church and other churches liable for the misconduct of clergy. Boy Scouts and the Department of Defense have faced lawsuits for failure to protect clients and employees.

Definitions have been hammered out in the workplace as corporations and school districts have been forced to understand the issue and its complexities and establish policies. Some of these key developments are outlined by Elaine Landau in her book, *Sexual*

---

[21] *The Book of Resolutions of The United Methodist Church, 2000*, (Nashville, TN: The United Methodist Publishing House, 2000) 141.

Harassment.[22] The AT&T communications giant, for example, developed a written policy against sexual harassment, indicating that words and actions without touch that are unwelcome or degrading are not appropriate.[23]

Further, sexual harassment included threats that sexual advances offered or rejected would influence personnel decisions regarding employment, wages, duties, and other conditions of employment.[24] Ultimately, laws are effective only to the extent that they are followed and enforced.

Thirty years later The United Methodist Church has done a lot of homework on the topic of sexual harassment. It has established a definition of sexual harassment.

> [Sexual harassment is defined as] any unwanted sexual comment, advance, or demand, either verbal or physical, that is reasonably perceived by the recipient as demeaning, intimidating, or coercive.... Sexual harassment is not limited to the creation of a hostile or abusive working environment resulting from discrimination on the basis of gender. Contrary to the nurturing community, sexual harassment creates improper, coercive, and abusive conditions wherever it occurs in society. Sexual harassment undermines the social goal of equal opportunity and the climate of mutual respect between men and women. Unwanted sexual attention is wrong and discriminatory. Sexual harassment interferes with the moral mission of the Church.[25]

The United Methodist Church also has expanded its definitions, describing sexual misconduct as a betrayal of trust that shows up in a

---

[22] Elaine Landau, *Sexual Harassment*, (New York: Walker and Company, 1993).

[23] The ATT policy defined sexual harassment as unwanted behaviors including "unwelcome flirtatious advances, propositions, continual or repeated verbal abuse of a sexual nature, graphic verbal commentaries about an individual's body, sexually degrading words to describe an individual." Elaine Landau, *Sexual Harassment*, (New York: Walker and Company, 1993), 38

[24] Ibid., 38.

[25] *The Book of Discipline of the United Methodist Church 2008*, (Nashville, TN: United Methodist Publishing House, 2008), ¶161I, 104-105.

"continuum of unwanted sexual or gender-directed behaviors." [26] These may include:

> child abuse, adult sexual abuse, harassment, rape or sexual assault, sexualized verbal comments or visuals, unwelcoming touching and advances, use of sexualized materials including pornography, stalking...[and] sexualized conduct to take advantage of the vulnerability of another. It includes criminal behaviors in some nations, states, or communities.[27]

Sexual harassment is a form of sexual misconduct. A description of power relationships is added to the 2008 definition. Generally within the church, clergy have been considered to have power, a concept that needs review. The study that generated this book shows that there are times when a clergywoman is in a less powerful position than a church member. Nevertheless, the introduction of power relationships changed the 2008 definition to say that sexual harassment includes words or actions "perceived by the recipient as demeaning, intimidating, or coercive," and also creation of "a hostile or abusive working environment."[28] The Social Principles of The United Methodist Church add that "Sexual harassment undermines the social goal of equal opportunity and the climate of mutual respect between men and women" and that it interferes with the mission of the church.[29]

In the intervening thirty years, each United Methodist annual conference has developed a policy for clergy. Each conference has

---

[26] *The Book of Resolutions of The United Methodist Church 2008* (Nashville, TN: The United Methodist Publishing House, 2008) 140.

[27] Ibid, 140.

[28] The full text of this statement reads: "Any unwanted sexual comment, advance or demand, either verbal or physical, that is reasonably perceived by the recipient as demeaning, intimidating, or coercive. Sexual harassment must be understood as an exploitation and abuse of a power relationship rather than as an exclusively sexual issue. Sexual harassment includes, but is not limited to, the creation of a hostile or abusive working environment resulting from discrimination on the basis of gender." *The Book of Discipline 2008*, ¶161I, 104.

[29] *The Book of Discipline 2008* ¶161I, 105.

been asked to educate local congregations and take protective measures such as running background checks on all clergy, child care workers, and staff. In spite of these changes, conferences have not developed policies on sexual misconduct for laity or church members towards clergywomen. This may be due, in part, because clergy want to keep their jobs: A denomination may not want a clergy person who sues a lay person.

While the church has analyzed the power that the office of clergy holds in relation to lay persons, the church has not fully come to terms with all the legal and moral responsibility it has with the combination of gender roles and clergy office. All too often men assume power, even to the point of abuse of women. So when men in congregations assume power in their relationships to clergywomen, issues need to be resolved with implementation of appropriate policies to protect clergywomen. We explore the complexities involved in protecting clergywomen.

Sexual abuse is defined by state laws, and these are enforceable. The definitions of sexual harassment used by the annual conferences are being shaped by the statements of the *Book of Discipline*. The conference definitions typically indicate that sexual harassment is "any sexually related behavior that is unwanted, offensive or which fails to respect the rights of others."[30] The widespread practice of establishing definitions and policies for clergy sexual misconduct is an outcome of coordinated efforts and work of the Commission on the Status and Role of Women together with the General Board of Higher Education and Ministry.

The United Methodist Church has referred to the Equal Employment Opportunity Commission for lists of unwanted behaviors that may include "unnecessary touching, pinching, patting or closeness; sexist remarks about a person's body or clothing...;

---

[30] "Sexual Ethics Policy for Clergy of the Oregon Idaho Annual Conference of The United Methodist Church," 2008.

sexually degrading words to describe a person…; and judging a person by looks or body instead of ability."[31]

One aspect of sexual harassment in its broadest sense has to do with pressure to be sexual. A person experiences sexual pressure when sexual harassment is difficult to refuse. This might be the case for a student who needs a class or a particular grade, or an employee who needs a job and a paycheck. Sexual harassment can span a wide spectrum of behaviors, ranging from obscene jokes to sexual assault. A supervisor or teacher may continually proposition or flirt with someone at work or at school.[32]

Sexual harassment is also sex discrimination, according to Catherine MacKinnon. In her research on sexual harassment and the workplace she defines sexual harassment as "the unwanted imposition of sexual requirements in the context of a relationship of unequal power."[33] Sexual harassment may be a one time encounter or a series of incidents at work.

Amherst High School in Amherst, Massachusetts, wrote a policy that listed many common actions as harassing behavior. These include:

> staring or leering with sexual overtones; spreading sexual gossip; unwanted sexual comments; pressure for sexual activity; and unwanted sexual comments; pressure for sexual activity; and unwanted physical contact of a sexual nature.[34]

Sexual harassment is not just about position, such as teacher-student or clergy-laity relations. Sexual harassment is about gender. Various school codes have identified that sexual harassment departs from an appropriate professional role between teacher and student. Landau writes, "Intimate relationships between professors and students are regarded with suspicion because they pose conflicts with

---

[31] Ibid.
[32] Ibid., 4.
[33] Catherine MacKinnon, *Sexual Harassment of Working Women*, (New Haven and London: Yale University Press, 1979), 1.
[34] Elaine Landau, 47.

faculty responsibilities and ethics...." Yet even more commonplace is sexual harassment of female students by male students.

When women's cultural roles lead to submissiveness, often young women grow up believing that it is appropriate for them to put up with sexual harassment. Typically it is all around. Elementary school girls and teenage girls rarely escape being harassed by boys. Landau points to studies showing that education in America traditionally served to reinforce women's dependency and reliance on authority. Some research findings underscore the fact that women are taught to be submissive. They learn that being "good" implies not acting but reacting, not trusting oneself but entrusting oneself to the authorities—parents, clergy, teachers—who promise reward.[35]

When a woman takes on a clergy leadership position, she may be unaware of apparently inherent skills she learned and ways she interacts with people. Even if she were aware, we cannot assume that church members are aware of gender dynamics.

Two other ethicists and researchers, Karen Lebacqz and Ronald Barton, authors of *Sex in the Parish*, state that when lay persons behave inappropriately toward their minister, male clergy tend to be concerned about others, but clergywomen feel personally at risk.

> Male pastors are concerned about protecting female parishioners from unprofessional advances. Female pastors are concerned about protecting themselves. The difference is striking. This difference is a key to the impact of sexism on sex in the parish.[36]

When Lebacqz and Barton inquired whether pastors had been sexually harassed, half of the clergywomen reported that they had been sexually harassed in the church.[37] As pastors were interviewed about their experiences with sexual harassment, their reports showed major differences between what women and men ministers

---

[35] Elaine Landau, 53.
[36] Karen Lebacqz and Ronald Barton, *Sex in the Parish*, (Louisville, Kentucky: Westminster/John Knox Press, 1991, 133.
[37] Karen Lebacqz and Ronald Barton, 135.

experienced. They observed the power of patterns of gender thinking that contribute to the way sexuality is perceived in the parish.

> In a culture in which women and men are not raised to be equal sexual initiators, men will think in terms of initiation of sexual activity and women will think in terms of response to initiation from outside....[38]

Lebacqz and Barton also found that although a small percentage of male clergy had some uncomfortable experiences with sexual harassment, "they had not experienced situations with the same level of fear, threat, and potential loss as those described by nearly half of the women respondents."[39] In dealing with gender and power issues in the church, the stakes are higher for clergywomen.

In order to explore power dynamics between clergy and laity, the church cannot look solely at the role and office of pastor. Gender is an important part of the equation. Sexism affects women in professional pastoral roles in the church.[40] The church does not have a tidy equation that can claim that the pastor is the perpetrator and the lay person is the victim. In order to understand misconduct and appropriate boundaries for behavior it is crucial to ask who has power and how gender is perceived. This demanding task will not likely be accomplished when the church is engaged in settling lawsuits.

Before 1973, the United States had no word for sexual harassment. Neither did the country have any laws concerning sexual harassment. Definitions and laws took shape differently in various nations. That is an important detail for this study. Two different legal forms of sexual harassment have emerged in the U.S. These are clarified by Abigail Saguay who describes one form of sexual harassment as the creation of a hostile environment and another as

---

[38] Ibid., 134
[39] Ibid., 136-137.
[40] Ibid., 139.

intimidation or enforced compliance with sexual advances in exchange for something that the victim needs.

1) creation of hostile environment
A boss or a colleague makes sexual jokes, unwanted sexual comments, demands for sex, or sexist insults. This is creates an abusive work environment.

2) *quid pro quo* sexual harassment

One person threatens another with loss or hardship if he/she does not comply with sexual advances.[41]

Employers are required to follow certain government rules. Secular employers can be sued for compensatory and punitive damages under Title VII of the Civil Rights Act of 1964, which makes it illegal to discriminate on the basis of race, color, or sex, or national origin.[42]

Churches are exempted from this form of accountability by the Civil Rights Act of 1964. Churches have sought legal protection under the clause of separation between church and state. Under this umbrella, churches also have the power to discriminate and exclude. Women may believe that their rights are protected by law, but it is their responsibility to understand the limitations and interpretations of the law when they work for a church.

The *Book of Resolutions of The United Methodist Church* contains a resolution called "Eradication of Sexual Harassment in The United Methodist Church and Society." By the year 2000 this was an eight page document with a description of legal and policy development in the U.S., a summary of efforts made by the church and additional sections about evolving international research and policy, why people should be concerned, and what they must do.[43] The 2008 resolution added a concluding section headed "A Vision of God's Hospitable

---

[41] Abigail C. Saguay, *What is Sexual Harassment?*, (Berkeley and Los Angeles: University of California Press, 2003) 2.
[42] Abigail C. Saguay, 6.
[43] *The Book of Resolutions of The United Methodist Church, 2000*, ¶31, 140-148.

Community" that set a theological tone saying, "Sexual harassment destroys community. This alienating, sinful behavior causes brokenness in relationships—the opposite of God's intention for us." It called on the community of the followers of Jesus to be "stewards of God's community of hospitality" where people celebrate "the presence of welcome, respect, and equality."[44] The church grounds its theology in these eloquent statements and calls for action.

In The United Methodist Church, ideally policies should be even-handed and fair toward clergywomen. Let's take a look at what is happening.

---

[44]*The Book of Resolutions of The United Methodist Church, 2008,* ¶2045, 139.

Can the Church Hold
Lay Perpetrators Accountable?   5

The first strategy for congregations to deal with harassment of clergywomen has been to ignore the problem and hope that perpetrators will stop their behavior or that clergywomen will leave. Neither course of action is acceptable.

With the present system of church law and administration, holding perpetrators of sexual harassment of clergywomen accountable is difficult, if not impossible. To understand why, we examine the consequences laid out for lay persons who engage in sexual harassment.

The procedures are ineffective in part because they cross lines and confuse boundaries of responsibility. There is no functioning system that consistently reprimands inappropriate harassing behavior by lay persons. For these reasons we now review procedures in The United Methodist Church for handling lay persons who perpetrate sexual harassment of clergywomen.

Clergywomen can file a complaint against a church member. Usually complaints are handled by committees, but there is a possibility, if the problem is not resolved, that a clergywoman can follow certain steps and the church will take a member to trial. We could examine records of church trials to see what happens, but if we do, here is the surprise: Trials of lay persons seem to exist in theory but not in practice, or they are kept confidential. It is difficult to locate records of trials of church members. My inquiry turned up only one record of a trial of a lay person over the past one hundred years, and that did not pertain to sexual harassment.[45]

---

[45] A 2005 search of the United Methodist Archives at Drew University in Madison, New Jersey produced no records. A 2010 archival search confirms this and revealed

If a charge of sexual harassment is pursued in a complaint, charges and an investigation, technically all records are open to proper church officials, the plaintiff and the respondent.[46] However they are kept private if the accused does not agree to make them public. If this happens, without having records the procedures, proceedings and cases cannot be reviewed, remembered historically, or given pause for reflection about what is to be learned about patterns with perpetrators and victims. There is no record to be examined to see if the church systematically upheld processes for justice. When trials are kept confidential, laity found guilty of engaging in sexual misconduct may lose their church leadership position or membership, but it still would be possible for them to pursue sexual misconduct in other congregations and other locations.

Records of a trial are kept by the secretary of the local church charge conference where the lay person is a member. Out of sight of the archives or the general church, they are obscured, if not totally inaccessible. A clergywoman may wish to protect her privacy because of potential shame and damage to her career involved in reporting incidents of sexual molestation or harassment. However, none of the privacy requirements prevent persons other than the plaintiff and respondent and those involved in the case from speaking out. Rumors and truth have a life of their own outside the judicial process.

In their interviews, most clergywoman felt that the annual conference and church leaders did not make clear the politics behind the processes the clergywomen were to follow. The church's first concern, in most circumstances, is to minimize the church's liability. The church annual conference has a role to protect the clergywoman and the parishioner at the same time that it is protecting itself. The church can control its media releases, whether a case is open or

one 2009 laity trial not related to sexual harassment. *The Relay Online*, email newsletter of the Greater New Jersey Conference of The United Methodist Church, May 2009, 5. Not available online at UMRelay.org.

[46] *The Book of Discipline of The United Methodist Church, 2008* (Nashville: The United Methodist Publishing House, 2008), ¶2706.5, 764 and ¶2714.7, 776.

closed, but it cannot control what is being said by the public in the church or the community, however accurate or inaccurate.

In the 1990s several highly publicized clergy trials led to changes in the process and in the list of chargeable offenses. New procedures were initiated and existing ones were clarified. Although the same basic procedures may apply for clergy or laity, one list of chargeable offenses and consequences is specifically addressed to clergy and another, slightly different list, to laity.[47]

The United Methodist Church has developed a list of offenses that can be grounds for official complaints, charges, trial, and expulsion. Gender discrimination was added in 2004. Of the ten offenses, at least five pertain to the topic of this book. These include sexual abuse, sexual misconduct, harassment, gender discrimination, and "relationships and /or behaviors that undermine the ministry of persons serving within an appointment.[48] Sexual harassment of a clergy person undermines a ministry. In cases of sexual harassment of clergywomen by a lay person, several charges might be filed together. As of 2011, the church did not yet have any public track record of prosecution of church members in church trials under these charges.

Whenever a clergywoman experiences sexual harassment, the situation is complicated. There are confusing twists and turns, lack of clarity and conflicts of interest in the mandated procedures for The United Methodist Church and its leaders and representatives. With such bold statements and policies on sexual harassment in place, it seems as though there should be no problem with filing a complaint and having it resolved. Wrong. Most clergywomen don't know how to file charges. Chargeable offenses are hard to pin down and document. It may be difficult to provide witnesses to the offenses. Even if the process were to work in the favor of the clergywoman who files a complaint, there are other problems.

---

[47] Laity are not charged for being "self-avowed practicing homosexuals" or for conducting holy unions.

[48] *The Book of Discipline of The United Methodist Church 2008* (Nashville, TN: The United Methodist Publishing House, 2008), ¶2702.3, 754.

When a complaint is filed, the district superintendent is instrumental to processing a case of sexual harassment of a clergywoman. In the job description for a district superintendent there is a conflict of interest. The district superintendent is supposed to provide support for the pastor (victim), the perpetrator, and the congregation of the perpetrator. All are under the jurisdiction of the district superintendent. The district superintendent has to maintain relationships with the people of the church and the pastor.

The pastor has to maintain relationships in the congregation, probably including relationships with family and friends of the perpetrator. When a pastor files charges against a lay person, he or she enters into an adversarial process. There are always critics in the congregation who feel that the pastor is not doing his or her job. This opens up opportunities for people to air their criticisms. If a complaint becomes formal, members of the congregation are likely to take sides and become involved in struggle and controversy, all requiring substantial time on the part of the district superintendent. The tension climbs, and the district superintendent and pastor have additional work dealing with conflict.

If a laity trial were held, it would create an upheaval, not only in the local church but in the broader United Methodist system. The district superintendent has responsibility to preside over the trial as a neutral party unless he or she hands this task over to another district superintendent. Quite possibly, relationships are too close within the church to be able to establish disinterested accountability. The district lay leader helps the district superintendent choose a committee on investigation. One wonders whether this task can be undertaken without bias.

If the victim is on the staff of a larger church, the pastor in charge works with the district superintendent. The clergywoman's judge at a trial might be her district superintendent who is her supervisor, evaluator, and who represents her employer. Her privacy is lost in the process of pursuing justice, and her pursuing a complaint might cost both her job and her career.

The procedures involved in filing a complaint and taking steps toward a trial are so complex that it is not likely that church members would want to go through such a complicated process. Technically, if an incident takes place and a lay person is charged, the church member might simply ignore church efforts to hold him or her accountable.

Until recently, there was no provision for the process to continue. The church did not define what to do with members who were accused of acting inappropriately with clergy and who dropped out of the process. The 2004 General Conference sealed this escape route by declaring that if a person fails to appear to deal with a complaint or trial, the processes may continue without his or her participation. Because taking a lay person to trial who is accused of being a perpetrator of sexual harassment is parallel in form to a clergy trial, one might anticipate that, as in the criminal and civil courts, cases would be brought forward in numbers related to the frequency of the incidents of sexual harassment. However laity trials just don't take place and probably shouldn't take place. We have seen only one public laity trial in modern United Methodism since the early 1900s.[49] To understand why, consider what is required for a trial.

A laity trial deals with a specific category of people—church members, otherwise known as professing members or lay persons. All the rules are written to deal with church members. There is no provision for lay persons who are constituents and not church members, a technical escape route which quickly permits some perpetrators who sexually harass clergywomen to get off the hook.

The steps for a clergywoman or anyone else with a complaint are very complicated. First, the procedures specify that a clergywoman should attempt to resolve the complaint on her own, or take the complaint to the district superintendent for assistance with resolving the problem. If this does not work, the clergywoman proceeds by preparing a written complaint. This should be done with utmost care

---

[49] Greater New Jersey Conference, 2009.

and professional assistance. A complaint is a technical term for a written document that describes the date, time, location, persons involved, and the incident. A legally constituted committee on investigation is appointed to review the complaint. The committee is appointed by the district superintendent.[50]

If a complaint is not resolved, a formal judicial procedure begins with filing written charges which face fresh hurdles. The original complaint is sent to the church legal counsel who prepares a judicial complaint and supporting material that is to be considered by the committee on investigation. The steps for resolution of the complaint are repeated. This time an unresolved complaint against a lay person is sent back to the pastor in charge of the local church, who, in this scenario, is the same person who filed the complaint in the first place. The committee on investigation may choose to dismiss the judicial complaint. It may refer other matters of concern to proper church officials. If the committee finds reasonable grounds, the committee can prepare a bill of charges and specifications for a trial.

A church trial is a very complex event that is modeled after a civil trial, with lawyers present, witnesses testifying, and points of church law argued.[51] When an investigation proceeds to the trial stage a court is convened. It is presumed that the trial will be held in the district of the charged lay person, although there is provision for the trial to be moved, upon request, to another district. In The United Methodist Church the annual conference, already dealing with limited fiscal resources, covers the cost of the trial, which may run from $75,000 to $200,000 depending on the security, investigation, witnesses and legal services needed. If a trial results in conviction, the trial court sets a penalty that may include removing the respondent from professing membership, suspending the perpetrator from holding office, or some lesser punishment. The punishment is not

---

[50] *The Book of Discipline of The United Methodist Church, 2004,* ¶2703.4, 722.
[51] *The Book of Discipline of the United Methodist Church, 2008,* ¶2714, 775-776.

specified in church law. The outcome will depend on what the jury believes at the conclusion of the trial.

To be sure, the process is long, complicated, and puts a clergywoman, the respondent, and her complaint in public view. The process is daunting for a clergywoman, already angry about being mistreated and still traumatized by the event, to pursue a complicated course of action by reporting the offense and making a complaint with no assurance that justice will be done.

Who would go through this cumbersome process if the ultimate outcome is that a church member loses his or her church membership? The church member doesn't have much to risk in exchange for inappropriate behavior. It would be easier for a perpetrator to withdraw from church membership and join another local church. What is to be gained by putting a lay member on trial when the only thing that can be taken away is their church membership? If there ever were a trial and conviction, and if the convicted church member were to move to another state or even another town, the record of the conviction would not follow. As one lawyer pointed out in an interview with me, "short of child abuse and murder, a church person can get away with highway robbery."[52]

What is the legal liability of church members for their treatment of their pastor? Does the local church have any of the financial or legal liability?[53] Congregations and annual conferences pay hefty insurance bills for liability coverage. If the local church had some financial liability, the congregation might think differently and seriously about receiving members. They might consider making sure

---

[52] *Eradication of Sexual Harassment,*
http:www.gcsrw.org/EradicationofSexualHarassment.aspx. See also Gail Murphy-Geiss, "Sexual harassment in The United Methodist Church, 2005," prepared by The General Commission on the Status and role of Women (Chicago, Il: The General Commission on the Status and Role of Women, The United Methodist Church, 2005).

[53] Military women who have experienced abuse in their workplace have filed suit against Defense Secretary Robert Gates and former Defense Secretary Donald Rumsfeld. Kimberly Hefling, "Veterans File Abuse Suit Against Comrades," *The Post and Courier*, Charleston SC, February 16, 2011.

that church members know their responsibilities, boundaries, and standards for behavior. Ultimately, this is where the church can do the most to deter sexual harassment of clergywomen.

One hoped for outcome of the church judicial process is to provide for healing if there has been significant disruption to the congregation. According to the *Book of Discipline*, the judicial process is intended to provide resolution for unresolved conflicts, support for victims, and reconciliation of all who are involved.[54] Since judicial proceedings are adversarial it is not clear how all of these things are to happen. In 2004, the General Conference added a provision that support be offered to a pastor who has been the victim of an offense.

Should the incident be taken to civil court or through church channels? In the United States, sexual harassment is a category of civil law, not criminal law. There is no imprisonment, probation, community service, rehabilitation, treatment or therapy imposed by a court for sexual harassment offenders. In civil court the penalty is financial.

Financial consequences, whether determined by civil courts or by contributors, have an important implication for United Methodists. The annual conference depends on the local churches for financial support called apportionments. The annual conference, in turn, is able to provide leadership, connectional resources, camps, campus ministries, and other joint programs that provide forms of witness and mission through common effort. The conference counts on each local church paying its fair share. When such conflict occurs in several churches, this can lead to contributions falling dramatically. This can lead to emergency cutbacks in conference staff, staff expense accounts, and program budgets. The costs of a trial cut into the church's ability to provide vital programs and services.

Clearly, the bishop and district superintendents and churches in the conference seek to minimize conflict in local churches. It is much cheaper, financially speaking, to move a clergywoman who has been

---

[54] *The Book of Discipline of The United Methodist Church, 2008*, ¶2701.8, 718

sexually harassed than it is to track down perpetrators and hold them accountable for inappropriate behavior, but that fails to handle the emotional costs involved in failing to stop inappropriate sexual behavior.

Where is the church's accountability to its clergywomen? Are United Methodist clergywomen being placed in suitable workplaces? Clearly clergywomen face workplace discrimination and danger on account of gender. Obviously the processes currently in place to provide oversight over the behavior of lay persons regarding sexual harassment of clergywomen are not adequate or effective.

If a clergywoman dares to seek justice, there are systemic reasons why the collective leaders of annual conferences would rather not challenge inappropriate behavior in a local congregation. It may place a clergywoman's career in jeopardy if she names injustice, files a complaint, or seeks justice. Given the imbalance between genders, the same might be true for injustices other than sexual harassment. Although remarkable strides have been made in naming and identifying sexual harassment, the issue of how the church can hold lay persons accountable for inappropriate behavior toward clergywomen has not been adequately addressed.

In spite of all the church laws, there is no true enforcement that holds lay persons accountable for sexual misconduct. This is why it is time to appeal for a new set of solutions. New processes can be drawn up and new policies and procedures implemented based on additional information and awareness about sexual harassment of clergywomen. We turn now to the results of the 2003 Survey of Clergywomen and Sexual Harassment in The United Methodist Church.

The Crisis Revealed 6

The 2003 Survey on Clergywomen and Sexual Harassment in The United Methodist Church in the U. S. revealed a variety of forms of sexual harassment and limited responses of the church. This chapter describes the survey and what clergywomen are telling us about their experiences with sexual harassment.[55]

The survey information was sent to 663 clergywomen.[56] A total of 215 clergywomen who came from all five U.S. regional Jurisdictions returned valid surveys. Thirty-six women thanked me for conducting this survey. Let's review the data.

The first section established demographic information. This survey did not show a correlation between ethnic/racial background and sexual harassment. This means that a woman of any ethnic or racial background could become a victim of sexual harassment. Geographically, the distribution was widespread. Three quarters of

---

[55] A website hosted this survey of clergywomen. Two postcards mailed a month apart invited women to take the survey, described how to access the website, and reminded them to take the survey. In order to discern the geographical distribution of sexual harassment the survey went to an equal number of women in all jurisdictions across the U.S. Beth A. Cooper, *Do No Harm: Sexual Harassment by Laity of United Methodist Clergywomen*, DMin. Dissertation, Wesley Theological Seminary, 2007. COSROW conducted a survey that confirmed the numbers of clergywomen who experienced sexual harassment. *Eradication of Sexual Harassment*, http:www.gcsrw.org/EradicationofSexualHarassment.aspx. See also Gail Murphy-Geiss, "Sexual Harassment in The United Methodist Church, 2005" (Chicago, Il: The General Commission on the Status and Role of Women, The United Methodist Church, 2005).

[56] Some of these people did not participate for various reasons. In addition to the 215 who took the survey, three responded that they did not want to take the survey. Twenty-one postcards came back as "return to sender," and thirteen women wanted to take the survey but had problems getting onto the internet. These thirty seven women did not take the survey.

the responses came from the Northeastern, North Central and Southeastern Jurisdictions.

Of the women who took this survey, most were European American, in their 50s, married or previously married, without children living at home. Their responses were not much different from the others. Ninety-one percent were working full time as clergy, and eighty-one percent were elders in full connection. Their experience in ministry ranged fairly evenly covering from five to over twenty years of service. Only 14% were serving their first appointment. The rest had been in ministry serving two, three, or four appointments, with 31% serving in five or more appointments.

The rest of the survey had to do with what women experienced in the areas of sexual harassment and sexual abuse in their work settings. The top four categories of most common forms of sexual harassment that women experienced in their work setting were these:

Received sexual comments	56%
Received unwelcome touching	48%
Publicly humiliated	42%
Felt fear in the work environment	41%

These statistics encourage people to ask what church work environments are like when nearly half of all clergywomen experience sexual comments, unwelcome touching, public humiliation, or fear.

Sexual harassment and sexual abuse in work settings

The survey asked, "Have you ever experienced the following while employed as a minister?" "If so, did you feel it happened because you were a woman?"

TABLE I

Experiences of Abuse

Type of Abuse	Percent who experienced this abuse	Percent who felt it happened because they were a woman
Received sexual comments	56%	90%
Received unwelcome touching	48%	90%
Publicly humiliated	42%	86%
Felt fear in the work environment	41%	65%
Been threatened	33%	74%
Person entered home uninvited	25%	19%
Called names	23%	NA
Stalked/followed	20%	76%
Been physically abused	13%	82%
Paycheck withheld	12%	48%
Tampered with mail	10%	38%
Family/friends threatened	10%	73%
Sexual pictures left in work environment	6%	58%
Pets hurt/poisoned	4%	33%
Experienced rape/attempted rape	3%	100%

Each of the perceived experiences of abuse was explored with additional questions. Who did this? To whom did you report the incident? First, let's look at the data as it tabulated in terms of percentages.

TABLE II

Sexual Comments in the Workplace

Sexual Comments in the Workplace.   56%

Who made these comments?

Parishioners	43%
Ministers	20%
Members of the community	7%
Combination/other	30%

Sexual Comments: Who did you tell about this?

Combination/other	40%
Other ministers	16%
Family	14%
Friends	13%
Church leadership	6%
Parishioners	4%
Community	2%

Sexual Comments: What action was taken?

None	59%
Combination/other	18%
No response	12%
Confronted the problem	11%

TABLE III

Unwelcome Touching in the Work Environment

Unwelcome touching in the work environment   **48%**

Who did this?

Parishioner	58%
Combination/other	21%
Minister	15%
Community	5%
No response	1%

Who did you tell?

Combination/other	38%
Family	15%
Friends	15%
Minister	15%
Church leadership	7%
Parishioner	6%
No response	4%
Community	1%

What action was taken?

None	53%
Combination/other	20%
Confronted the situation	13%
No response	11%
Filed a report/transferred	3%

TABLE IV

Have You Ever Been Humiliated in Public Gatherings?

Have you ever been humiliated in public gatherings? 42%

By Whom?

Parishioners	44%
Minister	32%
Combination/other	17%
Community	7%
No response	1%

What action was taken?

None	57%
Confronted the situation	20%
Combination/other	19%
Transferred	2%
No response	2%

TABLE V

<u>Have You Ever Felt Fear in the Work Environment?</u>

Have you ever felt fear in the work environment?   41%

Afraid of whom?

Community	28%
Parishioner	25%
Combination/other	17%
Minister	14%
Unknown	12%
No response	5%

Who did you tell?

No response	65%
Combination/other	22%
Minister	5%
Church leadership	5%
Friend	2%
Family	2%

What action was taken?

None	36%
Combination/other	28%
Confronted the issue	18%
Filed a report	9%
Transferred	5%
No response	5%

In the church setting entirely too much energy is spent dealing with inappropriateness in the workplace. These events distract from a pastor's focus on Christian ministry and her wellbeing in the workplace. Energizing power and better spiritual leadership could be unleashed if this were not necessary!

Who is doing these things to clergywomen? The survey also revealed that in eleven of the categories surveyed parishioners were the most frequent harassers. This table reviews categories indicating the percent of clergywomen who had this experience, followed by the percent of these incidents attributed to parishioners.

TABLE VI

Categories in which Parishioners Were the Most Frequent Harassers

1 Ever tampered with mail

2 Paycheck ever withheld

3 Ever stalked or inappropriately followed

4 Ever been threatened

5 Family or friends ever been threatened

6 Ever been physically abused

7 Ever received sexual comments

8 Ever received unwelcome touching

9 Person ever entered home uninvited

10 Sexual pictures ever left in work environment

11 Ever humiliated in public gatherings

Clergywomen usually were not able to identify the offenders of harassment involving several forms of harassment such as "pets ever hurt or poisoned" and "telephone hang ups." These are underhanded acts. The least frequently reported offender group, members of the "community," were identified most often for the categories "experienced rape or attempted rape" and "felt fear in work environment."

Survey respondents indicated that when they reported harassing incidents, nearly every time the most frequent response was that no action was taken. In only three kinds of situations, action usually was taken. These categories were "rape or attempted rape," "paycheck withheld" (confrontation and doing nothing were tied for top position) and "ever stalked or inappropriately followed." (See Table III).

Serious problems can result from lack of action in response to harassing incidents. Clergywomen may not trust church leaders. As this survey shows, clergywomen's concerns have been dismissed as not being significant or not worth time spent to resolve them. Clergywomen may have seen too many incidences where church leaders do not want to be bothered with gender issues. Even if clergywomen trust enough to report incidents and if they believe that they will not be dismissed, church leaders may not know what to do or how to follow through. If church leaders do not like conflict or are not good at confrontation, they may fail to act.

Sometimes other clergy are perpetrators of sexual harassment of clergywomen. Although the category of ministers was not most frequently named, numbers show that clergywomen cannot trust some of their clergy colleagues. For example, in the category "ever humiliated in public gatherings," although parishioners were named in 44% of incidences, ministers came in at a whopping 32%. Clergy offenses were lower when the abuse was more physical, yet clergy registered frequently as sexual/gender harassers in other types of abuse. A narrow reading indicates that clergywomen have a greater chance of being sexually harassed or abused by parishioners than male clergy. A broad interpretation indicates that male clergy participate in a church culture that does not reject outright "mild" forms of sexual harassment.

There is an age factor in the category for "repeated telephone hang-ups." Clergywomen in their forties and fifties experienced this form of harassment more frequently than other age groups.

Clergywomen were more likely to have experienced harassment if they had served more appointments. Clergywomen with two to four appointments were more likely to have experienced "being called names. Women who were not in their first appointment more frequently reported that they had experienced physical abuse. The two categories of unwelcome touching and feeling fear in the work environment also were correlated with longevity in ministry.

As long as a woman remains in ministry she is vulnerable to the possibility of experiencing incidents of physical abuse and gender harassment. We next explore what this information means for clergywomen and the church.

Understanding Clergywomen's Experience

7

Sexual misconduct is detrimental to the soul and well-being of the victim. Clergywomen are no exception. Grief, loss, anger, and shame may accompany the experience. Three percent of the clergywomen who took the survey were victims of rape or attempted rape. Even when it is hard to take a case to court, provide convincing evidence and win a judgment, women know that rape is a crime. In the case of rape, a sexual offense is clear and unambiguous. Women know when sexual harassment occurs.

Women's experiences are more confusing when it takes them a while to figure out what happened or when church leaders minimize or dismiss the implications or excuse perpetrators. Several women respondents in this survey were told that their experience was their own fault.

Sexual misconduct and gender harassment are complicated when a woman feels that something is terribly wrong or feels violated and does not have words to articulate the problem. It can be worse when people blame and judge the woman. Women hear put-downs and comments such as, "She's always complaining." "She is always a victim." "You can't rely on what she says. Where's the evidence?" "It's her word against his word." "I think we should drop it. It's not a big deal. She's just making a mountain out of a mole hill." "If she had a better attitude, I could sympathize with her, but she is always bringing up feminist issues. Her perspective is one-sided." "I really think that she is to blame. If she had only done ____, this wouldn't have happened."

When clergywomen experience sexual abuse that is not physical, the discovery that this is wrong is a discerning process which may not include instant awareness. The intuition of clergywomen may tell them that what they have experienced makes them feel bad. It raises their level of anxiety, discomfort and fear. It adds stress and puts them in a position of disharmony, if not conflict, with others. Yet hurts that aren't physical can be just as wrong or detrimental to the soul as physical wounds. The survey reports that when offenses were physical, women sought out action to terminate or redress the wrong-doing. When they were not physical, often women were left without help or support.

Clergywomen experience more emotional sexual harassment than physical sexual abuse. Why? Is this because church leaders are clear that physical sexual abuse is wrong? Has our culture agreed not to tolerate physical abuse? Of the two, emotional abuse is more ambiguous. Can we identify the wrongful behavior? One district superintendent pointed out, "What's hard to prove or be taken seriously about is when you don't want the hug because the last hug didn't feel right, or you know that he is trying to take advantage but all you have is your word."[57] There is more to emotional abuse than an action. The words, the look, the context and history all matter. Feelings may be doubted or considered a matter of interpretation. And how do you prove unwelcome touching, name calling, and sexual comments if there are no witnesses?

Four percent of the women who took the survey said that their pets had been hurt or poisoned. The person who hurts pets is threatening physical harm to the owner of the animal. Disturbed people use this psychological approach to create fear and threaten potential victims. Nine percent of the respondents indicated that their pets had been harmed or that they were victims of rape or attempted rape. A clergywoman may feel that the violation of sexual harassment defiles her call to ministry by defying who she is, what she represents and what she teaches. Horrific violence typically begins in a more common setting.

---

[57]Anonymous, interview 2 with author, 6 November, 2001, interview in person, notes.

One of the most widely used forms of harassment is name calling. The purpose of name calling is to shame people and take power away from them. Nearly one in four respondents who took this study had been called names. The free form of the survey gave the respondents space to give extemporaneous answers, and those who responded to this question provided ample examples of inappropriate names. All names that were mentioned had to do with female gender or sexuality--whore, slut, bitch, lesbo, lesbian, dyke, etc. Conversations, as well as the survey, revealed that name calling is not directly correlated to sexual orientation. Most women who took the survey were married or had been married.

Women don't have to do anything to be a target of sexism: Their gender alone makes them a target. Sexism degrades women because of their gender. Most of this violence is not visible, yet unstopped, it can escalate. Individual incidents of sexual harassment do not tell the whole story, but they do point out the direction.

In her book, *A Call to Hope: Living as Christians in a Violent Society,* Vern White claims that the violence we see and hear is like the tip of an iceberg.[58] Beneath the surface are two layers that support the visible violence and sexual harassment. One of these layers is the way an institution permits sexism to thrive in attitudes, behaviors, and traditions. Beneath this layer is another one of cultural sexism that rears children and youth with gender expectations. Most of us grow up with cultural education about power and dominance, competitiveness and authority for men, and expectations for women of submissiveness, sensitivity, nurturing and caring, domestic skills and having responsibility for tending relationships. In other words, there are cultural patterns that support gender violence.

For White, the visible violence is small compared to the enormous portion hidden from view that constitutes an underlying violence. When we see what happens to clergywomen, we may

---

[58] Vern White, *A Call to Hope: Living as Christians in a Violent Society* (New York: Friendship Press, 1997), 22.

assume that the abuse of women in the parish by parishioners may be much greater and that the church is unaware of, or covering up, an enormous problem. This metaphor leads us to examine what lies beneath the surface and out of sight in the church, and to review the assumptions of culture and style of church leadership that has brought us to this point. Cultural assumptions and attitudes have a long history.

From ancient times, most religious practices have been complicated by gender biases that have left women in a secondary position in relation to men. Gender concerns are present in debates about how biblical texts and their interpretations treat female authority and leadership. Gender discrimination is present in ethical teachings about sexuality, barrenness, childbirth, menstruation, abortion and parenting. Sexism is part of the culture in which the church exists. Because the church is responsive to the culture, sexism in the church is perpetuated by the church itself. Church culture has given preferential treatment to leadership styles that use hierarchy and dominance. Gradually this is changing. Openness to women's pains and concerns is helping to create communities where respect for persons is highly valued and where people learn to accept one another's differences.

When the church sets a good example and does not tolerate inappropriate behavior, the inappropriate behavior is less likely to occur. The church needs to give a clear message in order to stem the tide of abuse of clergywomen. If church members are inappropriate with clergy or other church members, and if such behavior is not stopped, others may imitate.

Clergy should not be inappropriate with or take advantage of parishioners. Such behavior is abusive. The United Methodist Church is learning to give a clear, decisive response to sexual harassment of parishioners. It also has policies for dealing with a clergy person who sexually harasses another clergy person. These policies get results. Sexual abuse or sexual harassment by a pastor is not allowed. Inappropriate exercise of ministerial office can be punished by removing the minister from his or her appointment. The church can take away a specific assignment, a career or credentials.

Without clear forms of accountability and enforcement for persons in the pews, the church does not teach or model the inappropriateness of sexually harassing clergywomen. There is a different standard at work. Typically there is no expectation that an offending lay person will face any consequences. If the issues are pressed, the church does not have effective ways for dealing with or untangling its mess of sexism and gender issues.

The outcome of the lack of consequences for perpetrators is that clergywomen do not have protection in the workplace. In general, clergywomen are unaware of the lack of right and protection that they experience by being employed in the church. Without solid backing from the church when sexual harassment occurs, what do clergywomen do? Some stay and some leave.

About 60% of clergywomen regularly deal with gender discrimination that contributes to depression.[59] Sixty percent of the women said their sleep was restless. Fifty-six percent felt tearful and more than one third (35%) said they "Could not shake off the stress even with help from family or friends." Women become frustrated with the appointive system and its lack of support. Clergywomen's rates of pay and promotion level off. They experience what is known as the "stained glass ceiling." The evidence points to systemic problems of sexism that lie behind the retention issue.

Women who continue in ordained ministry do so even though they are not safe from sexual harassment. One such clergywoman grew up in the Southeast Jurisdiction, married, went to seminary, and now is raising her family in this same area. Although she had received sexual comments that were inappropriate and had been threatened, she stayed because this was her home and she understood the culture.

---

[59] Constance Shehan and Marsha Wiggens Frame, "1995 Survey of 190 Ordained United Methodist Clergywomen, University of Colorado in Denver. Denver, CO. http: //news. ufl. edu/1999/06/09/clergy. Accessed 12 October 2006.

Another woman from the Western Jurisdiction moved because she could no longer "look the other way" at how women were being treated. When asked why she moved, she responded that God was calling her to a place where her gifts and services would be appreciated and used. This is a silent exodus, a course of action taken by many clergywomen.

Studies show that clergywomen and ethnic minority pastors leave The United Methodist Church at a higher rate than male clergy of European American descent. Studies of retention of United Methodist clergywomen were conducted in 1999 and again in 2010 by the Anna Howard Shaw Center in Boston.[60] The United Methodist Church has also traced a high rate of exodus of clergywomen from their profession, even 50% or more in thirteen annual conferences after ten years.[61]

More women are attending seminary and preparing for ministry than ever before. In some seminaries, women constitute more than half of the students in their class.[62] About half of ministers who are ordained are women. After the first ten years of service, the percentage of men who remain in ministry in a local church is significantly higher than the portion of clergywomen. Women leave the church for many different reasons that include raising children, juggling two careers of partners, and caring for older parents. Yet beyond all these reasons, some clergywomen indicated in interviews that trauma from sexual harassment or abuse was enough to motivate them to make the move to start life over again.

---

[60] Anna Howard Shaw Center, "2010 Study of Retention of United Methodist Clergywomen" Boston University School of Theology, Boston, MA, has not been released as of the publication of this book. www. bu. edu/sth/shaw/current-2010-womens-retention-study/.

[61] www. gcfa. org/PDFs/Gender2004. pdf. November 2, 2006.

[62] The Iliff School of Theology, for example, has enrolled women comprising 64% of masters degree, non-degree and certificate students. Letter from President David G. Trickett to Alumni. (Denver, CO: The Iliff School of Theology, 8 November, 2010.

Review the following 2004 tables that show the percent of clergywomen leaving parish ministry by the tenth year and the annual conferences who have the fewest clergywomen.[63]

TABLE VII

<u>Clergywomen Leaving Parish Ministry by the Tenth Year</u>

Conference	Percent
Mississippi	83.3%
Kentucky	66.7%
Western North Carolina	66.7%
North Alabama	60.0%
North Texas	60.0%
South Georgia	57.1%
Virginia	56.7%
Memphis	50.0%
New Mexico	50.0%
North Arkansas	50.0%
Northwest Texas	50.0%
Troy (New York)	50.0%
Wyoming (New York)	50.0%

---

[63] www. gcfa. org/PDFs/Gender2004. pdf. November 2, 2006.
www.bu.edu/sth/shaw/retention. Accessed 28 October, 2006.

TABLE VIII

Annual Conferences with the Fewest Clergywomen

Annual conferences with fewest clergywomen

In order from fewer to more clergywomen.

Memphis
Kentucky
Alabama-West Florida
Red Bird Missionary (Kentucky)
Rio Grande
North Alabama
Northwest Texas
Mississippi
South Georgia
Holston (Tennessee)
Western Pennsylvania
Arkansas
North Indiana
Central Pennsylvania
South Carolina

There is a correlation between the six annual conferences with the worst retention rates for clergywomen and the list of ten conferences with the fewest clergywomen. This suggests that these conferences may not be as conducive as others to promoting thriving ministry with clergywomen.

If the greatest hardships that clergy faced were cold, ice, and long distances, one might expect that clergywomen would not be able to fulfill parish responsibilities in remote areas of Alaska, Montana and North Dakota. Instead, the list of annual conferences which are among the most difficult for clergywomen to serve indicates a regional bias. One might ask if there are geographical correlations with the types of experiences of sexual harassment. This underlying layer may support forms of harassment that were not measured in this study. While this study did not show a regional difference, the retention rates indicate that this could be explored in more depth. This information about clergywomen opens the door for further discussion concerning how the church participates in dysfunctional systems that undermine its mission.

Sexual Harassment and Leadership Issues

8

The challenge before us is to understand the systemic gender issues and leadership styles in the church at work in dysfunctional ways in order to be able to identify points of change. Many conditions and complicated factors combine to allow the abuse of clergywomen. Social attitudes and cultural conditions, running like underground water deep and out of sight, imbedded in the culture, sustain the environment that allows the abuse of clergywomen.

The situation is grave. When the church fails to respond or take action and when that harassment is taken lightly, the culture of harassment is empowered. Overall, the church has failed to stop the abuse of clergywomen. When this happens, the church has fails to bear witness to God's love, to provide hospitality, to protect from harm, and to heal its own clergywomen. The church must tend to problems of sexual harassment of clergywomen in order to be able to advance its own mission.

Carol Becker, who wrote the book, *Leading Women: How Church Women Can Avoid Leadership Traps and Negotiate the Gender Maze*, claims that the church gives mixed messages. Church women in leadership are welcomed by pronouncements of inclusiveness, quotas to insure this and invitations to speak and be visible,

> on the other hand, they are made unwelcome, either explicitly or implicitly by habits of language that exclude them, by an entrenched male hierarchy in the clergy ranks, by male theological dogma and thinking,

and by an enduring fear of their sexuality that is the legacy of a patriarchal Christianity.[64]

These mixed messages are the soil in which ambivalence grows related to handling problems with sexual harassment of clergywomen.

This 2003 Survey of Clergywomen and Sexual Harassment in The United Methodist Church[65] revealed a communication gap between clergywomen and their supervisors. The clergywoman does not trust that she will be heard, understood, and affirmed by the person who evaluates her work and who is responsible for providing her with a job or requiring that she relocate. Just when she seeks support, the real possibility exists that she will be blamed for what happened, labeled a problem, and given negative marks on her professional record. Superintendents and other leaders are highly attuned to issues of liability and the possibility of lawsuits because new lawsuits for cases of clergy abuse of lay persons are filed virtually every year. In general, the rise in lawsuits has worked to the advantage of those who have been abused because leaders have become more sensitive to complaints. When the assets of the larger church are at stake, the subject gets attention.

Beliefs about gender are at the heart of attitudes and situations almost imperceptible to people who accept that "this is the way things are. Males insult other males using female gender terms such as "sissy" and "girl" to demean, taunt, and indicate weakness. Gender issues effect decisions made in economic downturn, when there are more clergy than jobs, and when full time jobs decrease and there is an increase in part time employment.[66] Women are paid less for the same work as men. Gender is a foundational factor present in the ways some laws are written and customs practiced.

---

[64] Carol Becker, *Leading Women How Church Women Can Avoid Leadership Traps and Negotiate the Gender Maze* (Nashville: Abingdon, 1996), 61-62.

[65] Beth Cooper, "Survey of Clergywomen and Sexual Harassment in The United Methodist Church," San Diego, CA: 2003.

[66] Paula D. Nesbitt, *Feminization of the Clergy in America*, 125.

This theme surfaced earlier in the discussion of separation of church and state. Separation of church and state provided the staying argument that caused the U.S. government to exempt churches from being required to provide women and other minorities with equal protection under the law. Authors Leta Gorham and Thomas Waitschies in the book, *But They Won't Talk to a Woman*, claim that "male clergy protect their positions of power in the Church…by hiding behind the protection of separation of Church and State that is part of our history here in the United States."[67]

A great range of women's experiences across the United States and within The United Methodist Church provides ample evidence of male privilege. To increase gender awareness, the Commission on the Status and Role of Women began paying attention to what happens in church meetings. They started tallying who speaks in meetings, who makes motions, who is chair and who is secretary. These statistics show that men assume leadership roles and control the conversation in meetings, and further, that women defer to them. Grown accustomed to positions of power, frequently men experience distress when a woman challenges their thinking or leadership. Due to social conditioning, both men and women often are unaware of ways that ordinary experiences and expectations still discriminate against female gender. Gender issues influence how clergywomen act and are acted upon as leaders. Gorman and Waitschies point out,

> Male clergy have been socialized to understand that it is their right to be in positions of power and that it is their responsibility to protect the women who are subservient to them. Female clergy have been socialized to accept the role of assistant to the one who is in power, the male clergy.[68]

Although clergywomen may claim that they are in charge, and although they may set their own schedule and guide church priorities,

[67] Leta Gorham and Thomas W. Waitschies, *But They Won't Talk to a Woman* (New York: University Press of America, 1998), 45.
[68] Ibid, 45.

gender dimensions are at work. This shows up in how clergywomen decide their priorities.

When clergywomen work in a local church, for whom do they work? Clergywomen may feel as though they have many bosses. All church members are helping to pay the clergy salary, and often they feel that they can ask the pastor to perform certain duties for the church, if for no other reason than that the church members don't want to do what needs to be done.

Usually clergywomen have grown up being socialized to please people. Women are acculturated to seek approval. When asked to do something by a member of the congregation, some clergywomen are inclined to feel that they must do it, even if their professional choice would be not to do it, or to do it differently. The clergywoman may end up feeling that she is not simply pastor in charge, but also working for specific members of the congregation, especially for certain men. Leadership training for women helps clergywomen to make professional judgments based on what they know and feel rather than choosing to please others.

Clergywomen need specific leadership qualities from their district superintendents. Clergywomen need district superintendents who know their churches well enough to understand the systems of each local church—to know which churches are healthy, the histories, personalities and reputations they have, positive and negative. This knowledge can help make an effective placement in an appointment so that the pastor who is sent to a congregation will be capable of dealing with dysfunction in the local church.

If a clergywoman believes that she can handle any challenge, this sense of confidence may not be sufficient to cover a situation in which the real risks are high. Clergywomen need to be aware of their own skills and abilities and their limitations in the face of inappropriate behavior. Failure to deal with a dysfunctional system in a local church may result in the bishop or district superintendents labeling the woman ineffective in her ministry. If her work comes to a crisis point when one or more church members have perpetuated inappropriate behavior, a clergywoman needs the financial ability and emotional courage to leave her job.

Clergywomen work long, hard hours. Often they do not receive positive feedback and thanks for their work. They deal with complicated human lives and need professional support. For professional health and survival, a clergywoman needs to have a support system faithful to her.

As tempting as it may be to turn to other clergy in the immediate clergy network or to expect support from a district superintendent, there are risks involved in doing this. Over a long career in ministry, sometimes one minister has shared problems with another minister. The one who was the listener and supporter may become a district superintendent. When that happens, the inside knowledge about the one who needed assistance to get through a difficult time can influence the professional opinion that the district superintendent has of the minister who shared in confidentiality. It can hurt the reputation of colleague who once sought emotional support. A district superintendent may make personnel decisions based on past information about a woman who was dealing with trauma, transition or crisis.

An additional risk to clergywomen is that in many professional situations, what counts in the long term is not what actually happened but how it has been interpreted and remembered and whose version is considered to be true. So for the clergywoman who has experienced sexual harassment, unfortunately, it is not always safe to share all the details. Because of this, clergywomen need to keep excellent documentation on their leadership, their conversations, e-mails, and accomplishments. Especially in a job where a clergywoman is often working alone, it is up to her to communicate with her supervisor about what she does, how she leads, and how she maintains appropriate boundaries. Just because a clergywoman works hard doesn't mean that her supervisor knows what she does, what she does well, and where her truth is more credible than other interpretations. These records need to show a pattern of maintaining clear and appropriate boundaries in relationships.

A third pitfall for clergywomen is that they have a tendency not to be realistic about the limitations of the system and what it can and can't do. They need to be aware of the terrain in which they do ministry. Many clergywomen have few recourses and remedies or support for dealing with sexual harassment other than processing it verbally with friends and allies and whoever will listen. So it can be helpful for clergywomen to be aware of how all this works, and that the church system currently in place, because of its inadequacy concerning holding laity accountable, does not know how to handle these situations or come to their aid. A key avenue for action, then, is to complain about real experiences. This may turn into chronic complaining and clergywomen may sound like victims, creating a pattern that clergywomen need to avoid. The church will punish these behaviors.

There is abundant evidence that clergywomen are not working on a level playing field in a gender-biased culture and a local church that discriminates in its practices. It would be easy for a clergywoman to complain all the time because of the frequent problems and inequities involved in being a clergywoman.

Being stuck in victimization complicates the situation and continues dysfunction. In the book, *Never Call Them Jerks*, Arthur Paul Boers writes:

> Seeing oneself as a victim inhibits growth. We refuse responsibility and attribute blame elsewhere. With such an attitude, we block our capacity to grow. Moreover, when we regard ourselves as victims, we often act destructively and hurt ourselves more.[69]

Professional coaching or counseling can help clergywomen process and move through specific trauma and also daily hardships

---

[69] Arthur Paul Boers, *Never Call Them Jerks* (Washington, DC: Alban Institute, 2002), 122.

that go along with being a woman in ministry. Healing through inner emotional and psychological work takes time, but when it happens, a woman regains her confidence and her voice.

Overcoming pain and wounding from sexual harassment has complications related to pain and suffering that is a normal part of life. Although there is no escape from pain and suffering or from the unpredictable aspects of life, there is an emotional difference between pain caused by wrongdoing and that of accidents and natural disasters which are commonly understood to be a painful but natural part of life. Victims of sexual harassment often are aware that they were selected as a target of prejudice. In other workplaces a woman could seek damages for what she has endured, but in the church, recourse against damages is very limited.

Harm that people do to one another adds a layer of wounding. In the case of sexual harassment of clergywomen, someone has used physical or emotional force to exert control and power based on gender privilege. It breaks covenant with God, with people being the highest and best they can be. It interferes with people living fulfilled and happy lives based on relationships grounded in unconditional love. To be born female, to feel that call from God for ordained ministry, and then to be limited by someone else's warped narrow-mindedness is stifling and limits the work of God that might have been possible.

Harm is compounded when these acts are committed in the name of God. Sometimes the person doing the harm believes that he or she is carrying out God's will, enforcing a religious teaching about keeping women in her place, or trying to teach the clergywoman a lesson. Occasionally, a key layman in a congregation decides that he must protect the facilities, worship, or programming from what he believes are dangers being introduced by a clergywoman, so he threatens or harms the minister. At a minimum, sexual and gender harassment of clergywomen in the workplace adds wounding because the clergywoman has believed that her work is ministry and the workplace is safe. The wounding is deeper when someone that she has trusted as a capable, responsible Christian leader breaks trust with that covenant relationship and causes harm.

Moving beyond wounding is multi-faceted and takes place in many ways. Interviews with hundreds of clergywomen gave me insight about how harassment and abuse changed their outlook. Being a victim in an incident is not the end of the story but rather part of a long process. The damage continues and hard work goes on and on. It isn't easy to "get over it." After being sexually harassed, women who normally would grow through an experience, learn from it, and integrate wisdom and faith experiences now see their ministry through the eyes of shame and wounding imposed on them. Some women that I interviewed still had not worked through their grief.

Clergywomen described to me the deep hurt they felt because people they knew were inappropriate with them. Inappropriate behavior disrupts and breaks work relationships and friendships. Violence may wrap the victim in shame. It is a silent, insidious, damaging process.

Where does a woman find protection and safety?

In the institution of the family, many people hold the perception that the family is there to protect you. What happens when family does not provide security?

In the U.S., as in most other nations, women aren't safe. In the United States, on the average, a woman is battered by a male partner once every seven seconds.[70] While the U.S. still has not adopted an amendment to the Constitution granting equal rights to women, and with violence against women still on the rise, the number of families experiencing domestic violence is increasing. Without intervention, some family members are not even aware of the ways they participate in physical and emotional violence. Violence can be an addictive

---

[70] Federal Bureau of Investigation, Crime Statistics. www.fbi.gov. "Domestic Violence Fact Sheet."
www.athealth.com/consumer/disorders/DomViolFacts.html. Accessed October 24, 2010. U.S. Department of Justice National Crime Victimization Survey, 1996.

behavior for which the whole person needs treatment such as is accomplished in recovery programs. When a perpetuator is in a good mood, he or she may be compassionate, understanding, and charming.

Bad relationship habits formed or used in a family setting can override and overpower a public or church setting. To illustrate, a mild mannered man might suddenly scream at a clergywoman. Members of a congregation may be aghast and silent on seeing how one of their members treats another family member, church member, or the pastor. The shock and surprise may mean that no one intervenes to stop inappropriate behavior in a public setting.

One clergywoman could not believe what happened to her. She helped a family through a funeral. She had prayed with family members, cried with them, and was there for an intimate, important passage with this family. Yet following all of this, what left her bewildered was that the husband of the deceased berated and humiliated her in a public gathering. He continued to put her down in meetings and after church services. Perhaps this could be excused by saying that this was a case of transference. Probably he was transferring his pain and grief of the death onto the clergywoman. That would be an excuse. He was degrading her as a woman, not disagreeing with her theology or the level of quality of her ministry. In seminary the clergywoman received education to prepare her to deal with people who thought or believed differently. She had no preparation to deal with a different personality that can emerge in a church member due to family system dynamics.

They never prepared me for the high amount of sexism that I have experienced in the system. I prayed with this man, and cared for him and his family. It was confusing to realize that I could not go back to that moment that I had to deal with the harm and the degradation that he was doing to me in the "now." I began to understand the confusion that a battered wife might feel when she has experienced one side of her "attacker" and then, at other times, she experiences the direct hit of being slapped physically, abused mentally, or berated spiritually.[71]

The church's domestic violence can be described using family and marriage images from scripture and theology. The New Testament describes the church as the bride and Christ as the bridegroom. Cultural gender roles can take what might be helpful and make it sexist. A layperson may mix the bride/groom image with cultural expectations and imagine that he is the groom in the church family and that the woman pastor or church member should obey and do what he says. I have seen members of congregations dislike and traumatize pastors—men and women. Members of churches may display their dislike for a pastor by avoiding, shunning, ignoring, or contradicting the pastor at every turn. Whether a pastor is male or female, church members may boss their pastor, emotionally batter, humiliate, embarrass, shout, or call the pastor names, but this happens more often to women because they are women.

Woman pastors may experience all these things, but at the core of the pain that she experiences is the knowledge that when the church ordains women, gives them opportunities, assigns them to places of responsibility, it isn't prepared to deal with the abuse that exists in local churches. Clergywomen typically keep the secret because they aspire to have a successful career and need to have a good record for their career moves.

Traumatizing behavior sets the stage for the victim to feel shame. It can be embarrassing to a clergyperson, highly educated, capable and prepared to lead a congregation, to be put in a position of not knowing where to go or what to do. Lack of action in response to sexual harassment or sexual misconduct only reinforces the behavior of a layperson that is getting away with inappropriate or criminal actions.

When I was a young person in church, one Sunday, during the closing hymn, "God Be With You Till We Meet Again," I watched a

---

[71] Anonymous, interview 1 by author, 16 June, 2001, interviewed in person, notes.

90

husband lift his hand and hit his wife so hard that it knocked her backward in the pew. I immediately looked up at the pulpit. From the look on the pastor's face, I knew he had witnessed what happened. I thought that for certain that somebody would say something about this behavior. Neither the pastor nor anyone in the congregation had anything to say to the husband.

Several years later that same pastor became a district superintendent. I often wondered whether, if a clergywoman under his appointment were experiencing unfair working practices in her appointment, he would come to her aid. In the case of the woman in his congregation, nothing was done--not a word, not an action, not even a look. It was as if nothing had occurred. In that vacuum, the church's integrity was compromised. The church needs its integrity in order to be authentic, faithful in discipleship to Jesus, and in witness to God's love.

The story of the church and its people, no matter how grim, is reality. Out of our stories, we grow our identity. We learn from our past. What we go through and how we interpret that through the lens of faith is the ground for our integrity, a strength needed for our faith journey. So our history is important and these clergywomen's stories are invaluable.

Many women who shared with me were concerned that their names would be revealed or that, for disclosing their stories, more harm would be done to them. Many clergywomen who had sought help from church leaders found that when the church processes were involved, they did not feel validated. Instead, the processes and people who came to their aid often continued the inequities of sexism by making assessments and concluding with negative judgments: "She needs anger management." "She is ineffective." "She was the one in charge and couldn't handle her assignment." Church leaders did not know enough about gender issues, violence, sexual harassment and abuse in the church to understand that anger and ineffectiveness can be by-products of the way the church has treated clergywomen.

When it comes to domestic violence, the batterer will not get help until he is forced to see that his behaviors are inexcusable. The same is true for issues around sexual harassment, harm, or unfairness: Until the church takes a stance of zero tolerance, people will continue to bully, harass, call names, gossip, and otherwise interfere with the ministry of clergywomen.

Churches are situated in the environment of a culture that is gender differentiated. Most of the time people participate in this culture unaware of their assumptions. Until men speak out and hold each other accountable instead of saying nothing or walking away, they hold on to gender privilege. Instead of preserving this aspect of culture, it is time to develop congregations that nurture healthy relationships.

In the same manner that a church knows the importance of protecting its investments and lowering risks of liability, it also must protect and create environments in which people will excel. Sexism that underlies this problem is an obstacle to the church's desire to have open hearts, open minds and open doors. The crisis in the treatment of clergywomen indicates a need for change. This crisis has also produced an exodus of women from ministry. We have shared the analysis and understanding. Now we share the stories.

The Long Tradition

9

The church has a long history of clergywomen who have not been cared for by the church. Some have stayed and some have left. Either way, clergywomen have paid, and continue to pay, a high price. The history of gender discrimination in the church underscores its effect on clergywomen and the church and the meaning of these choices. Despite having new policies and procedures, the church has not resolved its problems with gender discrimination. The church has not been there for clergywomen. The distance in years between then and now helps clarify how culture influences church behavior and the difficulty that a church has in rising above cultural limitations. It is time for the church to take leadership to prevent injustice against women and change our cultural patterns.

Rev. Dr. Anna Howard Shaw, 1847-1919, has been honored by Methodists as one of the first women ordained as a clergywoman. Her achievement came at a heavy price. She was the second woman to graduate from Boston Theological School. She described in her autobiography what it was like to encounter discrimination in theological school when she attended from 1877 to 1880. She was the only woman in her class with 42 young men. Before the first hour was over she realized that women theologians "paid heavily for the privilege of being women."[72]

> The young men of my class who were local pastors were given free accommodations in the dormitory, and their board, at a club formed for their assistance, cost each one of them

---

[72] Anna Howard Shaw, *The Story of a Pioneer* (Cleveland, Ohio: The Pilgrim Press, 1994), 83.

only one dollar and twenty-five cents a week. For me no such kindly provision was made.[73]

When Shaw was denied ordination by the New England Conference of the Methodist Episcopal Church she transferred her membership and was ordained in 1880 by the New York Conference of the Methodist Protestant Church. Her experience with seeking and being denied ordination in the Methodist Episcopal Church demonstrated that the denomination was not able to get beyond gender issues.

Since 1830 when Jerena Lee sought ordination, women in the United States have appealed for various clergy rights—the right to preach, to baptize, to pastor a congregation, to participate in General Conference, and to be elected a bishop. In 2006 the United Methodist Church celebrated only 50 years of full rights and full conference membership for clergywomen. To this day, only 3% of large congregations have a clergywoman senior pastor. Daily there are fresh examples of ongoing practices of sexism.

Before full clergy rights were granted to women, those called by God to ministry experienced discrimination and responded to it in a variety of ways. Some who felt the call faced totally closed doors. Others served as pastors in local churches. Stories of the trauma involved are difficult to find. Rejection is painful. Some people don't want to recall the pain and others fear being labeled for complaining. Regardless of the type of discrimination, it is a traumatic experience for a person to be called by God and be rejected by the institution that nurtured them to hear God's call.

One very special story about an early preaching woman who was rejected by the Methodist Episcopal Church (that preceded The United Methodist Church) is that of Sally Thompson. Cultural attitudes presumed that a woman's place was in the home, not in the pulpit. Thompson's story began with acceptance. In 1822 she traveled to a Methodist camp meeting at Smithfield, Rhode Island,

---

[73] Ibid.

where hundreds of people were praying, crying, and being moved by the work of the Holy Spirit at a spiritual revival.[74] As she mounted the preacher's stand to deliver a sermon, some in the audience thought she was out of place. Yet Thompson served churches for nine years. Her congregation accepted her pastoral leadership in the church. Then she was moved away from the Boston area, where she was known, loved, and supported, to a parish in the state of New York, where she was not known.

In her new parish a few people felt that women should not preach. Clearly, she could, however. When Sally Thompson spoke, she drew large crowds. She had an amazing gift for leading others to Christ.

Two clergymen decided to rid the church of this problem. They accused her of being "manly" and "out of place." The two men brought charges against her at the clergy session—serious charges. She was accused of evil speaking, immorality, and insubordination to the Methodist Church. When she prepared for her trial she could not even speak for herself because women weren't allowed to testify. This act alone would have confirmed that she was being insubordinate. The trial was held. She had to rely on friends and pastors to speak in her behalf. Despite the two extreme clergymen who led the prosecution against her, the committee of elders found Sally Thompson not guilty.

One of the two clergymen then announced that he would appeal her case to the Methodist Quarterly Meeting. Two months later, in August of 1830, she received a letter telling her that she had been excommunicated from her church on the grounds of insubordination. Because of this particular finding of insubordination, if any clergyman asked her to fill the pulpit, which was a common practice, he could be put on charges as well.[75] He

---

[74] Catherine A. Brekus, *Strangers and Pilgrims, Female Preaching in America, 1740-1845* (Chapel Hill: University of North Carolina Press, 1998), 267-268.
[75] Ibid., 270.

would be guilty by association. She was never allowed to preach in a Methodist church after that.

Anna Howard Shaw and Anna Oliver are both well known in the struggle for clergy rights for women in The United Methodist Church. Both applied for ordination in 1880. Anna Oliver received her Bachelors of Sacred Theology degree from Boston University in 1876. She was asked to pastor one troubled church after another. She went to serve where the men didn't want to go. Eventually she was honored with an invitation to speak before the New England Annual Conference.[76]

Anna Oliver and Anna Howard Shaw had profoundly different experiences with ordination and their careers. When Anna Howard Shaw was denied ordination by the Methodist Episcopal Church, she left and was ordained in the Methodist Protestant Church. Anna Oliver felt a strong call to stay in the Methodist Episcopal Church and continue the struggle so that one day other women could be ordained. Anna Oliver prayed and worked for change. She did not know that in her lifetime she would never see a woman ordained with full clergy membership in the denomination to which she gave her loyalty. Both routes were difficult emotionally, and both women continued to experience discrimination. Unfortunately, we don't have records that describe their feelings and reflections in the later years of their lives. Anna Howard Shaw's trauma may have provided motivating passion behind her choice to lead a campaign for the women's right to vote in the U.S.

Anna Oliver represents thousands of women who knocked at the church's door thinking that the faith community would be excited about God's call to them. Yet these women were denied ordination because God had created them female.

Life-changing moments such as these make women aware of the sexism in our culture and lead them to make new life choices. Some

---

[76] Mark Chaves, *Ordaining Women: Culture and Conflict in Religious Organizations* (Cambridge: Harvard University Press, 1997), 166.

women leave--emotionally, intellectually and physically—in pursuit of safety. They redirect their lives.

One woman, who was one of the first clergywomen in her annual conference, believes that it is harder to be a clergywoman now than when she was first ordained. When there were fewer women in the pulpit, her presence was not seen as a threat to people who did not want a clergywomen as long as they were not in her congregation. This early clergywoman also noted that church members in the 1970s had more structured parameters than we see today governing what is appropriate and inappropriate behavior when handling disagreement. Contemporary culture shows evidence that people have fewer conflict negotiation skills and more propensity to engage in rude, demeaning or harassing behavior. Finally, she has observed that when there were fewer clergywomen, the clergywomen felt a strong commitment to be there for each other to provide mutual support.

Today there is a perception that with more clergywomen serving local churches they face fewer struggles and don't need as much support. Instead clergywomen are facing difficult issues and handling them alone. Clergywomen still face a rude awakening every time they discover that they are breaking ground on women's issues.[77]

Movements that have taken giant strides forward also can lose ground. History has demonstrated that prejudice has a way of taking things backwards. When three branches joined to form The Methodist Church in 1939, the Methodist Protestant Church already had ordained clergywomen in its ranks. In order to close the merger deal and satisfy the Methodist Episcopal Church, South, and the Methodist Episcopal Church, the final documents did not allow women to have full clergy rights. Seventeen years passed before The Methodist Church granted women full clergy rights in 1956.[78]

Although clergywomen's rights may never be reversed, clergywomen still face unequal working conditions in The United

[77] Anonymous, interview 7 with author, 8 January 2003, interview in person, notes.
[78] Patricia J. Thompson, *Courageous Past, Bold Future* (Nashville: General Board of Higher Education, 2006), 21-28.

Methodist Church today. Over fifty-five years after women first received full clergy rights in The Methodist Church, clergywomen do not receive protection from abuse in The United Methodist Church. This is a time to be vigilant on behalf of clergywomen. There is work to be done.

Do No Harm

10

In seeking fresh directions to solve the many problems that cluster around the sexual harassment of clergywomen by lay persons, one resource available to The United Methodist Church is the first of its three General Rules.[79] The General Rules provided simple and clear guidance to early Methodists. They have been updated to be easy for us to remember now: do no harm, do good, and stay in love with God.[80] The injunction to "do no harm," also a watchword of the medical profession, supplements Jesus' great commandment to do to others as we would want them to do to us. In this combination the church has a powerful foundation for training people in the intent and character of Christian living. We will explore resistance to change and strategies for leadership. We will recommend processes that can help make the church a safer place.

In the U.S. a backlash against women's rights fits a pattern. Movements for human rights typically take one hundred years or more to change cultural attitudes. About thirty or forty years after the movement emerges there is a time when the changes are visible and starting to approach the tilting point to become adopted by the culture. A backlash emerges that desires to hold on to the way things have been. In the case of clergywomen, as the portion of United Methodist congregations served by clergywomen increases, the level of conflict increases. The interviews for the survey demonstrated this backlash effect and increase in hostility toward clergywomen. We are seeing some gradual changes in response to this crisis.

---

[79]The General Rules, created by John Wesley, were established to guide Methodists in Christian living and adopted in the American colonies by the Methodist Episcopal Church in 1784.

[80] The full text of the General Rules is longer. *The Book of Discipline of The United Methodist Church 2008*, op. cit., ¶103, 73-74.

The United Methodist Church stands in opposition to sexual harassment, yet the church has not been good about protecting its clergywomen. It is time for the whole church to genuinely care about women. These women are mothers, sisters, wives, daughters, members of the community, strangers and clergy who come in every variety. In any parish a clergywoman is at risk of being sexually harassed. This is not tolerable. Since the church ordains women, it should provide them with adequate working conditions.

United Methodists have a legacy of leading change on certain social issues relating to expressions of equality and human rights in the church and the culture. United Methodists are bound to disagree on the subject of how clergywomen should be treated. However, when United Methodists are divided in opinion, the first General Rule of John Wesley remains a point of unity, and a connecting point for addressing the problem of sexual harassment of clergywomen.

The church needs thoughtful leadership when perpetrators describe their actions as choices made to protect others. Clergywomen interviewed for this study believed that perpetrators thought that they had the right to inflict harm to protect others. God was on their side and they had to teach somebody a lesson.

Typical ethical thinking allows people to do some harm if the result is for the greater good. Simply teaching, "Do no harm" is not enough, nor is enforcing penalties an adequate response. A three part approach might help the church deal with the fundamental issues behind the abuse of clergywomen:

1. Engage people in thinking through gender roles and stereotypes.
2. Develop awareness of the role of culture in influencing Christian thought and practice.
3. Explore biblical teachings that lead beyond dichotomized thinking about gender to a broader understanding of equal participation in the reign of God in church and society.

The church needs to keep its legislation current, policies in place, and leaders and members informed. Education about sexual harassment can include training for children and youth. Youth and adults in confirmation classes learn what it means to become a member of the United Methodist Church. To this we now add what the church expects about not harming others. As Christian disciples we need our energy, creativity, and work focused on bringing into fruition God's love in action. When we allow sexual harassment or abuse within the church, we cause harm that distracts us from our mission and hurts relationships. If we say one thing and do another, we are not being congruent as Christians. Our message needs to lead people to discover the joy of Christian living as a disciple of Jesus.

Making recommendations for systematic changes and procedures may be easy, but issues about gender will produce resistance.. Resistance may come from men who "protest too much" because they have been taking advantage of women for years and have no desire to stop. Key men in congregations may still use dominance over women to control them and to control a congregation. Some objections may come from clergywomen who have led the way to bring clergy perpetrators of sexual abuse to justice. They may fear that the new thrust will take attention away from the violations of professional behavior in circumstances when clergy are predators. Changes in understanding the power of laypersons that mistreat clergywomen will produce conflict when a congregation stands up against abusive power.

Resolving the problem of abuse of clergywomen begins with basics: People consider how they would want to be treated and treat others that way. It would make a difference if people could accept their woman pastor as a leader, cloaked with the church's authority, able to be a servant for Jesus Christ and not be objectified by others for their own gratification. But it isn't this simple. Sometimes clergy are not good leaders. They may dominate and control or disrespect lay persons. These behaviors break relationships.

People who attend church also spend their week influenced by cultural expectations and social pressures. They have absorbed assumptions about gender passed from generation to generation. Just as it is difficult for people in recovery to "kick the habit," it is hard for people with dysfunctional behavior to cultivate healthy ways of relating or to ask what fears from within are driving their behaviors.

There is power in self-reflection that can improve daily living and enhance lines of communication and improve the ways we interact with each other. Change is scary. People may fear the chaos that comes with loss of control, with change in routine. There are advantageous ways of going about introducing change.

In the book, *Leading Women: How Church Women Can Avoid Leadership Traps and Negotiate the Gender Maze*, Carol Becker lists ten processes needed for change related to leadership of church women. These are important in order to move to more specific actions.

Ten Factors Needed for Authentic Change

One   Reflection comes first, then action.

Two   Women and men must acknowledge each other.

Three   Sexism, racism, and other prejudices must be named and addressed.

Four   Women and men must be together in the same work setting.

Five   We all need more education.

Six   Power must be understood and used differently.

Seven   Theological issues must be addressed.

Eight   Inclusive language will help.

Nine   New models are required.

Ten   Individual change is not enough. Systems must change.[81]

Carol Becker gives us a good start, but the church needs to focus and strengthen what this guidance means. To make changes, the

---

[81] Carol E. Becker, *Leading Women How Church Women Can Avoid Leadership Traps and Negotiate the Gender Maze* (Nashville: Abingdon, 1996), 175-180.

church must develop a comprehensive training program on laity sexual abuse and harassment of clergy for use at all levels of the church's structure. Annual conferences need to adopt and implement a policy on sexual and gender harassment. Local churches have an important role. A model code of ethics, a "Covenant," provided at the end of this book, is a tool for educating local churches. Actions must be specific in areas such as these.

Ten Recommendations for General Church Action

1. Conduct studies to evaluate progress in incidents of sexual harassment of clergywomen.
2. Provide training for bishops, district superintendents and other church leaders.
3. Distribute educational materials for congregations
4. Schedule teams to help congregations implement changes.
5. Follow guidelines for actions when a woman experiences sexual harassment or violence in the church.
6. Sponsor a national hotline with trained staff for clergy who experience such violence.
7. Implement strategies both for leaving women in safe churches and for moving them to other churches.
8. Set up an independent website to document incidents, the depth and scope of the problem, so that better procedures can be established.
9. Give legal assistance, counseling and safe spaces to clergy who experience harassment or violence at the hands of laity.
10. Discuss and respond to the issue of how to hold volunteers accountable knowing that what happens to clergywomen also happens to lay women.

Michael Foucault, a French philosopher and social theorist, has examined successful institutions and the processes they used to change from unhealthy to healthy systems. He describes different forms of power, including the power of truth and the power to disseminate knowledge of truth. When a person grasps new information that increases awareness, he or she is empowered. When the same person shares this with others, the power extends beyond individual awareness to group awareness.[82] What is hard to accept is that the power to judge can so easily override the power of truth. It is easier for people to hear criticism and judgment than to hear truth and disseminate knowledge.

When there is not a balance between active listening and conscious decision making, there is no consideration for those who are not making the decisions. Our culture has a long history of not expecting women to participate substantially in decision making processes outside the home. Often people are unaware of the social bias that listens to men more than women.

The United Methodist Church has monitored its meetings, Annual Conferences and General Conferences. Men speak more often than women do. Studies support that this is learned behavior, developed in the early years of life. The process of socialization that leads boys to speak out more than girls is visible at the elementary school level.[83]

When a system punishes people who become aware of a new truth and disseminate this knowledge, it is because there is a bias or entrenched injustice in the old system. Ann Wilson Schaef and Diane Fassel, authors of *The Addictive Organization,* show that "all systems call for behaviors and processes from those within the system that are consistent with the system. Systems subtly and explicitly reward people exhibiting these behaviors."[84] Something internal has to change in order to change the outcome.

What changes the system is a dynamic of "tribal justice," according to Foucault, in which a community remembers its vision and recites the memory of its vision, values and truths. The community pays attention to the habits and behaviors that have evolved that are not consistent with the vision, stops reinforcing

---

[82] Michael Foucault, *Power/ Knowledge: Selected Interviews and other Writings* (New York: Pantheon Books, 1980), 33-35.

[83] Ron Scrimgeour, "Gender bias in the Classroom?" *Research Education* 52, Spring, 1993. www.scre.ac.uk/rie/n152scrimgeour.html. Accessed 6 April 2007.

[84] Ann Wilson Schaef and Diane Fassel, *The Addictive Organization* (Lanham: The University Press of America, Inc., 1998), 70.

these, and the community agrees not to tolerate them. The behaviors are not accepted. This is the heart of the approach to systemic change that could help The United Methodist Church.

The church became comfortable with a system in which men exercised power over women in the church. Like the boys in the classroom who became accustomed to having privileges of voice and power, men in congregations have become comfortable with having voice, power, and privilege of gender, including over clergywomen.

One way to subvert the power of the culture would be for the church to see itself as a tribe, or subculture, with its own vision, values and truths. By recalling this core of Christian living, the church could become more aware of how it has harbored behaviors that mistreat women. Using this truth, the church can stop reinforcing behavior that assaults clergywomen. Remembering its values and truths, the church can show respect to its clergywomen and expect women to be treated fairly.

Cultural Participation in Sexual Harassment 11

All of us live in the context of a culture. In these surroundings, we make choices every day, some consciously and some unconsciously, out of habit, that are based on our understandings of what is expected of us. This chapter explores how sexual harassment works in the context of our culture and also provides stories that show how easy it is for us to use unexamined words and behaviors. One key to change is making ourselves more aware of the patterns, the complications, and the interrelationships all around us that make up the climate that has failed to stop sexual harassment.

Typically, when a man does not want a clergywoman as a pastor, he has cultural tools that give him an advantage. Because of a bias built into the culture he knows how to dominate and insist on his way. When a man dominates by using abusive techniques ranging from name calling to physical assault, he uses the language and techniques he may have learned as a child, seen on TV, heard in the locker room, and used in a male-dominated workplace. Sometimes a woman uses such behavior to emotionally abuse another woman. Some people simply never question the right of men or women to be abusive.

Clergywomen experience more emotional sexual harassment than physical sexual abuse. Perhaps church leaders are clear that physical sexual abuse is wrong. Perhaps our culture has agreed not to tolerate physical abuse. Emotional abuse is more ambiguous. Perhaps it is difficult to identify the wrongful behavior. Emotional abuse is more than an action. The words, the look, the context and history all matter. It is reasonable to wonder how a person can prove unwelcome touching, name calling, and sexual comments if there are no witnesses or if witnesses didn't notice it or had a different interpretation of the same events. Ambiguity is an obstacle to clear action. In making interpretations, women can be an obstacle to other women.

Several women that I interviewed said that the worst obstacles to their ministry were created by women, not men. One clergywoman on her way into ministry was assigned a woman pastor to be her mentor. The mentoring clergywomen could not comprehend and did not want to hear stories of the difficulties faced by the younger woman because, as one of the early clergywomen, she perceived her hurts, scars, and pains as being worse than everyone else's. The clergywoman entering ministry said:

> I was wrong to think that all clergywomen are there for each other. I didn't realize it in the beginning, but over time I realized that she could never let me be paid a compliment when others would try to let her know what I was doing. She could only criticize and remind me that the younger generation would never have it as bad as the women before.[85]

Lay women in the church have also participated in the process of hurting clergywomen and undermining their authority. A clergywoman shared what happened when she first moved into the parsonage. She couldn't wait until she met the new church people. Men of the congregation struck up conversations with her as they unloaded the truck and carried her belongings into the parsonage. She found two or three women in the corner of one room commenting on how bad her furniture looked. They said that they hoped that the damage to the furniture wasn't the result of her housekeeping. One of the women came up to her and asked her why she wasn't married. Another woman from the church commented, "It's a shame that you are single. The parsonage is just going to be wasted!" Women can be inhumane to one another.

---

[85] Anonymous, interview 312 with author, 28 November 2006, San Diego, CA, telephone interview, notes.

Yet another way women participate in undermining clergywomen is when they witness clergy abuse or gender harassment and remain silent. In her the book, *Woman's Inhumanity to Woman*, Phyllis Tressler points out how women may use silence to punish. She describes how two or more women may create a negative environment by using staring or silence, and by ignoring another. She links using silence as punishment as a response to a woman "whose words, ideas, physical appearance [and] sexuality, threaten and challenge them."

> Sometimes, women fall silent as a way of punishing any woman who expresses herself directly, openly, regardless of what view she expresses. The directness itself seems to challenge women's enforced/preferred style of indirect expression and indirect "backtalk."[86]

Women who have been raised not to talk back and not to be direct have developed an arsenal of weapons that undermine authority using passive resistance. Men can also be indirect.

A clergywoman was appointed to a congregation that didn't want her. The congregation told church leaders not to send them a woman pastor, but one was sent to the congregation anyway. Within a month or two, one of the male leaders of the congregation made a pass at her. She told him gently, but with authority, that she was not interested. Her place was to be the pastor and this also meant that she was his pastor.

Apparently her "no" did not mean no. A couple of weeks went by, and he tried another approach. This time, to honor her professional boundaries, she was blunt and to the point. Then he told members of the congregation that their pastor had hurt his feelings. The congregation did not know the whole story, but because they had a general bias against the clergywoman, they rallied around him.

When she went to the Staff Parish Relations Committee about the matter, the committee did not believe that this man had come on to her. They thought that she must have done something to produce

---

[86] Phyllis Tressler, *Woman's Inhumanity to Woman* (New York: Plume, 2002), 144.

these actions. The pastor thought that at least she would have understanding support of the women who served on the committee. Instead, what she received when she questioned them were comments like, "What do you expect when you enter a male occupation?" "Don't you like it when men give you attention? What is wrong with you?" This clergywoman left the local church because the leaders of the congregation were not supportive but added insult to injury. She was moved and replaced by a pastor who had a wife and three children. The clergywoman felt that the church leaders reinforced the congregation's bias against women.[87] After this win for the congregation, the challenge likely would be even more difficult for a woman pastor in the future.

As the proportion of clergywomen increases in relation to men in ministry, more gender problems emerge. Women entering the occupation have no idea of the importance of support for one another. Often clergywomen will be critiqued as weak if they share their troubles with church leaders, so the support of a peer professional can be crucial when a woman is dealing with discrimination on account of gender. Clergywomen need to network to help those who are in trouble. The most effective support comes when clergywomen form a support group and meet regularly.

A social backlash against clergywomen is alive and well. The authors of *Clergywomen, An Uphill Calling*, point out "that when the percentage of women becomes 30%, a backlash develops against women, which intensifies as the number of women increases further.[88] United Methodists have reached that point in some areas. This has resulted in drastic losses of women from local church ministry.

In the book, *Ethics and Spiritual Care*, Karen Lebaqcz and Joseph Driskill cite a report that asserts that mainline churches are failing

---

[87] Anonymous, interview 191 with author, 14 May 2004, San Diego, CA, telephone interview, notes.

[88] Barbara Brown Zikmund, Adair T. Lummis, and Patricia Mei Yin Chang , *Clergywomen An Uphill Calling* (Louisville, Kentucky: Westminster Knox Press, 1998), 105.

women and men, not by neglecting spirituality in general, but by neglecting feminine and feminist dimensions of spirituality in particular.[89] In *Defecting In Place*, three women scholars and church leaders report results of a national survey on how women with feminist leanings deal with their spirituality. Over 50% of the respondents from every mainline Protestant denomination said that they "often felt alienated" from their churches and denominations.[90]

In his book, *Clergy Killers*, Lloyd Rediger wrote about spiritual abuse and how this may occur when lay people are inappropriate with clergy. Noting that one out of four pastors leaves ministry, Rediger raised questions. If the church removes approximately 5% who suffer from problems, including mental illness, that means that twenty percent of the total number of departing clergy leave for other reasons. This is a high dropout rate.

In this study, Rediger did not press on to explore the impact of the hatred of women, sexual abuse, or sexual harassment. He did not examine gender issues in the dynamics of church life. Many women, driven out of ministry by church politics, have been declared mentally unstable. It is incredibly hard for clergy to pastor a local church widely known for chewing up and spitting out its pastors, whether they are men or women. We need to ask what is going on in congregations. Who will hold congregations accountable for their meanness, fear, and hate toward their pastors?[91]

Attitudes about gender roles, what is appropriate and not appropriate, drive the problems behind gender harassment of clergywomen. A retired pastor wrote a letter to the editor of *Circuit West*, a monthly newspaper of the California-Pacific Conference of The United Methodist Church. He noted that Bishop Mary Ann

---

[89] Karen Lebacqz and Joseph D. Driskill, *Ethics and Spiritual Care* (Nashville: Abingdon Press, 2000), 99.

[90] Miriam Therese Winter, Adiar Lummis, and Allison Strokes, *Defecting in Place; Women Claiming Responsibility for Their Own Spiritual Lives* (New York: Crossroad, 1994), 51.

[91] Lloyd Rediger, *Clergy Killers* (Louisville, KY: Westminster John Knox Press, 1997), 5.

Swenson, an avid cyclist who daily rides to work, frequently had her picture taken wearing shorts or riding a bike. He said that he was sick and tired of seeing her portrayed this way and he wanted her to be seen in a more professional role. He suggested that it would be nice to see her in a dress from time to time.[92]   If the same paper had shown frequent photos of a male bishop wearing a sweat suit or bicycle shorts, riding a bicycle, probably the bishop would be appreciated for being strong, athletic leader who set an example for living a healthy lifestyle.

This author is typical of people who are not aware of their own gender bias in dealing with women as colleagues. If this lack of awareness of gender bias can be published regarding a bishop, it signals that the same bias is prevalent in the local church. If this can happen to a bishop, it can happen to any clergywoman.

The United Methodist Church agreed to give ordained clergywomen full rights in 1956, but it has not given them equality or safe working conditions. Since 1988 the United Methodist Church has maintained an active resolution about sexual harassment in the *Book of Resolutions*. This is not enough to correct the problems. Rules and regulations are only as good as the cultural attitudes that back them.

Hard at work on the issue of gender is the Commission of the Status and Role of Women (COSROW), formed in 1972 to advocate for women. COSROW monitors gender issues in the church. COSROW has been working all across the church to educate and to break down the barriers of sexism in the church. The Commission was formed with the hope and dream that every agency and church related to the United Methodist denomination would grow in sensitivity and awareness on gender issues. The Commission desires to help the church reach a new plane in gender equality. COSROW has focused its work on Safe Sanctuaries. As helpful as this program

---

[92] *Circuit West*, Cal-Pac Annual Conference, The United Methodist Church, November, 2006, 3.

is, it does not fully address how to handle volunteers who engage in sexual harassment.

One big step to help the church might be for each church to write up its standards, similar to samples provided in the appendix of this book, and to give each new church member a copy of the congregation's "Covenant for Zero Tolerance of Sexual Harassment" or its "Code of Conduct." These documents could be displayed in every congregation. They could be posted in church offices, sanctuaries, gathering places and websites. While there is no way to enforce good behavior, peer expectations can establish standards and norms for behavior in the life of a congregation. If a congregation does not follow through on the process of establishing standards and norms, its work on sexual harassment will not be taken seriously.

At the very least, the church can speak against sexual harassment and take action when clergywomen are harassed. If not, the church ends up reinforcing what it doesn't want and the church becomes a part of the problem. How can the church turn the tide around? It is time to look at the iceberg of sexual harassment and get to the stuff underneath the surface. It is not enough to name the wrongdoing. The church must decide what it will not tolerate. Leaders, pastors, and members of the church who look within themselves and find different ways to handle fear and hate can make a difference. The "Safe Sanctuaries" program, designed to protect children and church members, is a model for the kind of in-depth change in policies and procedures needed to protect clergywomen.

Work environments for women are changing in other areas of employment. This may inspire local congregations and annual conferences to face the depth and scope of the problem, document it and establish procedures, sanctions, counseling, hotlines, legal assistance and safe spaces for clergy who experience harassment or violence at the hands of congregants. Churches should examine the protocols on secular workplace protections for its employees as a baseline for protecting their clergy. The context of national and international law must be addressed. Churches should revise and rewrite policies that discriminate on matters of race and gender. Churches can advocate on behalf of women to change state and federal policies on sexual harassment.

We can learn from other nations. Abigail Saguay believes that various international perspectives on sexual harassment can be summarized in three ways. She says that the first way is to see sexual harassment as violence against women. Taken from this perspective, sexual harassment is a crime committed with intent to hurt another. A second way is to see sexual harassment as a lack of equality. It is discrimination perpetuated on a minority. Yet a third way observes that sexual harassment reduces work productivity. More work is accomplished in places where there is no sexual harassment.[93] The three belong together. The latter perspective, which focuses only on work and not on the harm done to people, is detrimental.

Just because the United States has focused on work productivity doesn't mean that the church cannot address all three perspectives on sexual harassment. We turn now to solutions.

---

[93] Abigual Saguay, *What Is Sexual Harassment? From Capitol Hill to the Sorbonne* (Berkeley, CA: University of California Press, 2003) 2-8, 17.

The Search for Solutions 12

There is room for the church to be a more effective caring community. If the church can change and provide a safe place for clergywomen, it can lobby and educate in the public arena for practices that would help prevent sexual harassment and sexual assault. It can look beyond financial penalties to care about the hearts and lives of the people harmed and wounded by sexual harassment.

Clergywomen can have a role in solving problems of sexual harassment. They need training about ways they can work with criminal and civil law on their side. Some laws can be used effectively by clergywomen. It is lawful to arrest a person for breaking and entering. It is lawful to report and prosecute a rape. It is lawful to report stalking, tampering with mail, or verbal threats of physical harm.

Clergywomen need to be able, without penalty, to refuse appointments in parishes in which their lives are threatened. Some parishes are more dangerous than others, but there is no parish in today's world where a clergywoman is not at risk of being sexually harassed or finding herself dealing with unfair working conditions. It bears repetition because this is so important to know, that one out of every two clergywomen has had one or more experiences of sexual harassment in their church workplace. We are breaking the silence.

Seminaries need to be part of the solution. Seminaries have trained clergy to handle theological differences, however, they have not trained pastors to handle the ways gender prejudice interferes with congregational life. They could introduce students to the topic of sexual harassment, both by clergy and by lay persons. Students could be taught how to write a formal complaint and where to file it to press charges. Even if the complaints do not result in prosecutions, they do help to confront perpetuators with the consequences of their behavior. Seminaries could train student mentors for internships so that men and women in hosting congregations learn that certain actions will not be tolerated. Seminaries could train women in points of law about where to go in cases of sexual harassment. The seminary, too, might be established as a setting in which sexual harassment is not tolerated. The seminary could provide for women a community with support and nurture.

Annual conferences have an important role for United Methodists. Clergy do not belong to a local church but to the annual conference. Conferences need to take care of their own members. During the period of provisional membership, new clergy could continue to learn about handling sexual harassment. Incoming clergy can learn how to call in parishioners' homes, how to meet people at the office, and what behavior is appropriate for conversation or touch. New clergy can learn how to report inappropriate behavior.

Each annual conference needs to undertake leadership training of its bishop, district superintendents, pastors, church officers, and church members. For most clergywomen who reported incidents of sexual harassment to the district superintendent or other leaders beyond the local church, leaders did nothing to help them. This does not build confidence or trust. Hopefully with new training sessions on sexual harassment, that may be changing. District superintendents still need information on sexual harassment of clergywomen by laity. Some are now receiving training to follow new procedures adopted by the General Conference of The United Methodist Church. The church needs to have updated policies and procedures in place in each annual conference that will guard confidentiality and protect a clergywoman's status and employment.

As an outcome of advocacy for clergywomen, the 2008 General Conference adopted two policies. The clergy session of every annual conference is to adopt a "comprehensive policy for handling sexual and gender harassment of clergy when lay persons are the perpetrators."[94]   The new policy will offer guidance to the local church, provide for support of the pastor and care of church members, and provide direction about how to care for and to all parties involved, the findings and the settlement. Establishing policies and plans for handling problems will go a long way toward making conferences more aware of the need to resolve conflicts of interest in handling these cases.

United Methodist Men stepped forward to take leadership in the arena of education and prevention of sexual harassment. They added to their responsibilities that they will "Cultivate leadership among men for a policy of no tolerance of sexual harassment in family, church, workplace and society."[95]

Debates in the legislative committees at the 2008 General Conference showed where the resistance to change is strongest and pointed out the issues that will require education in the years ahead. As the debate came to a head in the section on Ordained Ministry, various leaders stood to make the case that sexual harassment by lay persons is, in fact, an occupational hazard to clergywomen, and that Boards of Ordained Ministry should be informing and training local congregations how to minimize sexual harassment. With a general lack of awareness of the crisis involved, the sense of the room was that existing policies on sexual harassment are adequate to care for any problems that clergywomen might face.

In the section on the Local Church, proposed new legislation that would have required the congregation to deal with sexual harassment by lay persons was handily voted down by a large majority. One church leader who wanted the proposal defeated explained tongue in cheek that if the sponsors wanted the church to pass that kind of legislation they would need to get the issues aired on Oprah Winfrey's TV show. He seemed to be speaking an important truth.

Up to this point, The United Methodist Church has focused on stopping sexual harassment by clergy. It has put in place effective

---

[94] *The Book of Discipline of The United Methodist Church 2008*, ¶605.8, 374.
[95] Ibid. ¶2302.2f, 694.

leadership education and training, deterrents, and administrative policies. The church is attempting to stop the bleeding of millions of dollars in lawsuits that have stemmed from clergy sexual misconduct.

Until the church steps forward with leadership to establish a church wide policy of zero tolerance of sexual harassment by lay persons as well, the task is being only partially addressed. The church may try to protect itself against litigation instead of fully being the spiritual body of Christ in mission for its people. Either the church needs to step forward and address the problem of sexual harassment of clergywomen by laity or, quite possibly, it will need to respond to lawsuits from clergywomen. In the interim, there is plenty of room for all involved to work on solutions.

Clergywomen may want to ask how much harassment they can tolerate. Clergywomen may pray and discern where their call lies and what they can realistically do in the environment to which they have been sent. The world doesn't need more victims but rather more empowered people not willing to be oppressed. Clergywomen need to find out if their state has hate crime laws or not. They need to know whether leaders in their annual conference will or will not take seriously the issues and process around sexual harassment. If not, reporting an incident will only add harm to a clergywoman's career. She might be better off to exit her job. If an incident involves anything beyond sexual harassment, clergywomen need to be in touch with the police on matters of assault or any other criminal action. Clergywomen need to have a support network. It is a wise step for a clergywoman to form or join a group of clergywomen.

Depending on the degree of seriousness of an incident of inappropriate behavior, no one should fail to take seriously the threat of harm. If she finds herself in such a situation, a clergywoman needs to weigh all options and to be sure that she is protected legally and sheltered from harm. It is critical to document and keep documenting incidents. It is important for clergywomen to use safety precautions, especially when there is a threat of harm or danger. It is advisable for a pastor to leave a counseling room door ajar, have a witness present for business conversations, lock church doors when she is in the building alone, or keep a dog if she is being stalked. If a clergywoman has a family, her children need to be her first priority and be kept safe at all costs.

Clearly, local churches have work to do to keep clergy and parishioners as safe as possible. Lay people and clergy need to understand how family systems work. Karen McClintock writes in her book *Sexual Shame: An Urgent Call To Healing,* "[C]hurch leaders have become more and more aware that individuals in congregations act out unfinished issues from their families of origin..."[96] Individuals can and will use their church as an extended family. For every church that has been established for a generation or more probably there is a matriarch or patriarch, and often both, who model and monitor congregation behavior. The health of a congregation and its ability to solve problems and resolve ordinary crises that come with living may well depend on the mental, emotional, and spiritual health of the people in power. People learn patterns for living, positive and negative. They feel comfortable with what they know because they know what to expect and have developed ways to cope. They carry patterns from families into the church. If the members know how to work beyond their past, they will want a church to do that, too. If the members are stuck in old habits, they will want a church to protect and preserve their habits.

Churches are places where people seek God's guidance and help and strength for their lives. People want to feel safe and able to handle problems in need of grace, kindness, forgiveness and healing. Dr. Karen McClintock writes that all too often, families carry secrets and sexual shame. Some people come looking for places where their secrets can be kept hidden, but not all.

Still others seek a grace-filled place that will heal their feelings of shame. Most congregations abound with secrets and plenty of shame. Those who have grown up in similar environments feel at home in

---

[96] Karen A. McClintock, *Sexual Shame: An Urgent Call to Healing* (Minneapolis: Fortress Press, 2001), 79.

congregations that have secrets and shame.[97] The dynamics of congregations, therefore, often reflect the patterns of behavior that are comfortable to the people and that feel familiar. Some people are looking for healthy discussion, openness, and healing.

Dealing with problems of everyday life is different from dealing with problems that come from unhealthy human behavior. Jealousy, the need to control, and obsessions are unhealthy. Anger can be inappropriate. Prejudice can pass from generation to generation. It is time to examine the depth and severity of sexism in the foundations of the life and practices of each congregation. The church may want what is comfortable, but that may not be what is needed.

Change can occur aided by an open heart, depth of faith, and trust in the wideness of God's love. I remember a man who did not want me for his pastor. All the women in his life served him. His relationships with his mother, his wife, and his daughters centered around satisfying his needs with meals, care, and attention. I assured him that I was not there to gain power over his life but to remind him of the importance of his spirituality. I asked him if he thought that God was narrow minded and limited enough so as not to be able to use women to spread the Gospel and to lead others to a closer relationship with Christ. I asked him to remain open to further conversations and to realize that I would not have a deep, lower voice in the pulpit, and that I would probably do things a little differently. He did not quit the church. I was able to be his pastor through some significant times in his life.

A girl grew up in a church in which the only pastor she knew was a woman. When the clergywoman was moved, a man was sent to pastor. One day after Sunday service the young girl told her parents that she did not like the pastor because he was a man. How easily we become attached to habit, to what is familiar and comfortable! If we truly understand the call to be Christian, we must also understand that the Gospel calls us to move beyond what is comfortable.

---

[97] Ibid., 79.

Unconditional love and grace are more than events or passing moments in life. We must live love-filled and grace-filled. We must live beyond what we fear, and move on to what John Wesley called perfection, the life-long task of perfecting our ability to love as God does.

One of my friends who grew up Catholic in a church that does not ordain women came to a church service that I was leading. We met after the service and went out for lunch. I enjoyed her family and her kids as well. One day, several weeks later, my friend called to tell me what happened. She had entered the play room where her five year old daughter was playing. The girl had placed her stuffed animals in chairs, taken a loaf of bread from the kitchen when her mother didn't notice, and set the bread in front of her little congregation. She broke the bread and gave each one of the stuffed animals a piece of the bread. When her mother asked her what she was doing, she said that she was offering the body of Christ to her friends. She added that she was going to be a woman priest.

When my friend saw her little girl operating outside of the box of prejudice, she began to ask herself the question, "Why can't women officiate over Communion? Isn't God bigger than any church doctrine?"

I sometimes wonder what happened to the girl. Did she conform to the teaching that women can't be ordained in her church? Did God lay a special call in her life? What was her call? How did the family react? Was she given space to explore what God was calling her to be? Would the call be stronger than any obstacle of prejudice or any act of harassment? Asking the questions indicates an increasing awareness of the way our experiences and culture shape our beliefs. Sociologist Mark Chavis observes that "denominations are embedded in different cultural environments and these differences affect denominations' formal roles about women." He adds that women's roles and women's ordination have become "key markers of a denomination's cultural location."[98]

Gender prejudice and sexual harassment are bound up with cultural location, family systems, shame, power, dominance, and personal experiences. These forms of prejudice and abuse can lead to dislocation, distrust, and breakdown of relationships, safety, and community. They can disrupt relationships and take away from focus on spiritual growth and worship. When the church suffers under these circumstances its work and mission suffer.

Until we overcome these adversities in our communities of faith, the church will founder. The church must change in order to be what it is meant to be--a safe sanctuary, a place where all God's people truly are welcomed.

---

[98]Mark Chaves, *Ordinary Women: Culture and Conflict in Religious Organizations*, 39-40.

A Call to Action

The time has come for action. There are many things that the general church, clergywomen, conference leaders, and lay persons can do. A ten-point agenda for the general church has been laid out on page 103. Already you have taken the step of becoming aware of the issues. Sharing your awareness is crucial. Here are helpful suggestions for clergywomen, conference leaders, and lay persons. As problems of sexual harassment of clergywomen enter into the consciousness of the church, other actions can be defined and steps taken.

What annual conference leaders can do

Conference leaders need to be thorough in processing complaints of sexual harassment. Up to now, there have been too many times when United Methodist clergywomen who have been harassed went to church leaders for help and nothing was done. Persons holding the office of bishop and district superintendent often are overworked. This does not exempt leaders from following through the required steps and procedures of the annual conference and *The Book of Discipline* when a United Methodist clergywoman brings a complaint of sexual harassment.

1. *The district superintendent or bishop should be caring, thorough and helpful in protecting clergy who have been harassed.* A clergywoman's safety cannot be compromised. When a church leader has a conflict of interest, is biased, or cannot handle the situation, it is still his/her responsibility to extend the care of The United Methodist Church to a clergy member who has been sexually harassed, to find someone who can do this, and see that due process is followed.

2. *Conference leaders can assess and know their congregations.* One of the most effective ways to ensure a reduction in sexual harassment of

clergywomen is for official church leaders to understand the congregations under their charge. Before appointing a clergywoman, educate a congregation as needed. Offer training meetings to help people explore, discuss and deal with gender differences, stereotypes, and expectations. Give congregations tools for learning about sexism. Teach appropriate behavior.

3. *Conference leaders can give a clear message that sexual harassment is not tolerated and will not be tolerated in The United Methodist Church.* Perpetrators of sexual harassment engage in this behavior when they believe that they can get away with it. Research shows that when communities have zero tolerance towards sexual harassment and when appropriate expectations, guidelines, policies and roles are applied, sexual harassment is minimized. This creates a climate of openness for talk about gender inequalities without shame or put downs. Prevention is the most effective way to deal with sexual harassment.

4. *Conference leaders can learn more about gender inequality and sexism.* Understand that sexual harassment is not the victim's fault. Conference leaders should not expect a clergywoman, by herself, to stop sexual harassment being perpetrated against her or in her congregation or clean up the mess in a setting where sexual harassment has been occurring. Church leaders who have never walked in a woman's shoes may not understand from the inside how the threat of sexual harassment makes a clergywoman vulnerable. Clergywomen can be encouraged to step forward to stop sexual harassment at its earliest indicators. Annual Conference leaders must press on to learn about sexism, gender inequality, and cultural norms that compromise the church's commitment to equality and justice.

5. *Conference leaders can learn from the retention rates of clergywomen in their own conference.* The datedness of the surveys and studies show an urgent need for updated and more comprehensive studies of women in ministry. These studies should be scheduled and remedies prescribed and implemented.

What a lay member can do

1. *Lay persons may keep learning about issues related to gender equality.* Local churches may be participating in sexism, taking advantage of gender roles, and pursuing unexamined patterns that leave women vulnerable. How the church handles these issues speaks volumes and makes room for negative behavior to be acceptable and tolerated.

2. *Lay members can ask themselves how they function in family systems and how church family members treat others.* How are men treated? How are women treated? How do people treat someone who has fallen out of grace? How are new people treated? How do members of a congregation treat those who come to worship and seekers who come to learn about Christianity?

3. *Lay members can reaffirm and implement choices of the denomination.* As United Methodists, our policy making groups have affirmed that God calls women to be clergy. Clergywomen are given the rights and privileges of that sacred office. We believe that God expects us to show respect for all persons. Each local church should be aware of what it means to be a caring, compassionate sanctuary and how this translates in practice when a clergywoman is their pastor. It is appropriate to celebrate the many ways in which the whole church has helped women answer God's call to ministry and how this opens doors for women and daughters in the congregation.

4. *Lay persons can oppose violence against women in their community.* Emotional and physical violence is all too commonly part of a family's experience. Consequently it is important for the church to be involved in the community, calling attention to domestic violence month, volunteering at shelters or food programs, and using available creative means both within and outside the church to share the message that violence is never right.

5. *Lay persons can lead and participate in training programs on sexual misconduct that are part of Bible studies, and Sunday school curriculum, instructing all ages from kindergarten through older adult.* Committees can sponsor learning events about gender inequality. These programs help people who have different values, anger management issues, or

religious understandings that harbor attitudes of entitlement used to justify sexual harassment. Lay persons can commit to participate in church trainings and guidelines on how to create safe congregations.

What a clergywoman can do

When sexual harassment occurs, the most important thing that a clergywoman can do to reduce the likelihood of another incident is to tell someone about the sexual harassment. When a clergywoman puts up with sexual harassment because she believes that this person is a parishioner in need of ministry, she further enables a person who is harassing. This maintains an environment for harassment. While prayer and love are appropriate, incidents of sexual harassment break the pastoral relationship with the perpetrator. It does not work to think that a clergywoman can love or pray someone through to the other side of such misbehavior. It is also a mistake for a clergywoman to think that she can process her way through anger, grief and anguish by herself. Because abuse in any situation at any level of intimidation is never right, she should not tolerate inappropriateness bur rather set boundaries. Clergywomen may follow these guidelines:

1. *A clergywoman can tell someone she trusts.* A clergywoman should not go alone to the office of a church leader to confront this person or go by herself to a police station to report an incident. A clergywoman should avoid setting up a situation in which her word may be pitted against another person's word. An advocate, a witness who can help document what is said and agreed upon, is of utmost importance.

2. *A clergywoman can document every incident of harassment,* every meeting with any church official and law enforcement officer as to what was said, the timeline, and what agreements are reached. A clergywoman's record can document what occurs, patterns, changes, and escalation.

3. *A clergywoman can make a concerted effort not to put herself in harm's way.* The measures needed depend on the level and intensity of the harassment. If this means moving to another appointment, it is

important to do so. Violence of any kind is likely to escalate. A clergywoman should know herself and discern when and if it is appropriate to ask for a move. It is important for a clergywoman to trust her inner voice. Intuition is a valuable tool to help sense danger. Clergywomen need to be aware that, even with the best intentions, sexual harassment can happen to anyone.

4. *A clergywoman can use the process that the church has established to be used when sexual harassment occurs.* The system is there to ensure justice and fairness, although that may not happen. If you are a clergywoman you will want to acquaint yourself with the processes outlined by *The Book of Discipline*,[99] but start taking steps using your annual conference guidelines. Know that sometimes leaders do not follow these processes. If you are subjected to sexual harassment, pray and be wise about the outcome that you desire. It is up to you to decide what you want to do in the way of formal or informal response.

5. *A clergywoman can lessen her vulnerability.* Know and trust what you feel. Become familiar with your specific church's family system and the operative cultural norms about behavior with women held by the family leaders. As local congregation guidelines are written, and as policies and relationships are being cultivated and formed, train your church leaders to understand, apply and rely on *The Book of Discipline* and the Annual Conference guidelines and policies. Keep your own behavior above reproach, question or doubt. Be as safe as you can at all times. Know the laws about hate crimes, sexual harassment, and crimes against women in your state.

Sexual harassment of clergywomen must stop. The church cannot tolerate a gray area or false belief that cushions entitlement. Gender discrimination cannot be implied or practiced. The church has made a great start and the journey has been substantial, but we still have a long way to go for all to understand that even though culture does not stop at church doors, sexual harassment will not be tolerated. Although sexual harassment reduces work productivity in the church,

---

[99] *The Book of Discipline of the United Methodist Church 2008*, 750-781.

the church has a wider view of compassion and concern for people and healthy relationships. Sexual harassment harms.

The church can make a difference. The church can embody change and help our laws and culture protect women and all victims of sexual harassment. One excellent way to make sure that sexual harassment does not occur is to engage every person in doing his or her part to make sure that sexual harassment is never a subject for jokes, to move beyond doubt when hearing about sexual harassment, and to ensure that policies are in place and enforced to ensure a just, quick, and fair process. To do this honors the whole body of Christ.

Ultimately, the church cannot hide from the problem of sexual harassment in its many forms. When the church knows the pervasiveness of the problem and the damage being done it can no longer hide behind not knowing. The integrity of the church depends on its ability to correct the problem and establish a reputation for being trustworthy. Anything less subverts the gospel. Being a community of faith that lives as Jesus taught is all about caring for one another and transforming the world by the way we live. The message to the church is urgent: do no harm. It is past time to move beyond the stained glass ceiling.

Epilogue 14

Bishop Sally Dyck

Driving home from church one Sunday afternoon, I was listening to a popular radio show which has made Minnesota famous. On his weekly show, the storyteller has replaced the Lutheran minister in his mythical town with a woman, Pastor Liz, and in this episode he was describing her as "tall and beautiful." I was thinking about this book as I was listening and tried to remember how he had described the previous pastor, a male; tall and handsome?

Pastor Liz was going on vacation in this episode but before she did, she had to have her car serviced. The men at the garage were quite interested in what she would be doing on vacation. "Are you going to see your boyfriend?" they asked her. She told them that just as soon as she got a boyfriend they would be the first to know. Community people are always a little curious about the local clergy so I didn't think too much about this part of the story as they inquired into her personal life but noted how often people assume they can pry into clergy's personal lives as if it's assumed they are meant to be open books.

But before Pastor Liz left for vacation, she stopped to see an elderly man who was dying in the hospital. She went in and seeing him alone, she curled up on the bed beside him, granting him the pleasure of dying with a smile on his lips, the storyteller said. I couldn't believe the storyteller would describe her actions like this. Crawling up on the bed with a parishioner is a chargeable offense!

Evidently she realizes this—or better put, the storyteller realizes this—and Pastor Liz gets off the bed after the elderly man dies so that she's sitting in a chair when the man's family comes into the room. I was growing more and more uncomfortable with the direction that this storyteller was taking the character of Pastor Liz.

But it got worse.

Pastor Liz left the hospital and drove to North Dakota to visit a clergywoman friend for her vacation. Her friend's husband had recently left her. They were going to go to Seattle to find him but instead went to a hot springs by themselves in a nearby state. Since none of the other guests were using the hot springs, they had it to themselves and they spent the time lying naked next to each other for hours in total relaxation. There were no sexual implications between the two women but the storyteller seemed to relish the image of the two women, enjoying themselves in naked abandon as the just desserts of two overworked clergy. The storyteller seemed to think he was giving a great gift of luxury to these clergywomen but it smacked more of a titillating foray into his own imagination about these two clergywomen.

While a few months before I was pleased that he had made the new pastor in his mythical town a woman, now I was angry and disgusted with him. The messages he was sending to good church people—and some listeners who just put up with the church-y part of his show—were all wrong, perpetuating misconceptions and expectations that many of us in the church have long tried to eliminate.

One of the reasons that I was pleased that he had made the pastor of the mythical town a woman was because it would "normalize" having a woman pastor, especially in some communities where they have either not had one or still have some resistance toward women in ministry. But now, in addition to "normalizing" the clergy's inappropriate behavior toward a parishioner, he was "normalizing" laity's "right" to inquire, comment on, and fantasize about the personal lives, bodies and sexuality of clergywomen. This "normalization" is what feeds the cultural context in which sexual harassment occurs toward clergywomen.

This book, *Under the Stained Glass Ceiling: Sexual Harassment of United Methodist Clergywomen by Laity*, suggests that we need to become more aware of how clergywomen are vulnerable to harassment in the church and what creates the environment for harassment. When there is little or no boundary that prevents laity's assumptions and expectations that they can inquire about, comment on, and fantasize about clergywomen's bodies, sexuality, and personal lives, an environment is created in the church (and community) that the woman is "fair game" for inappropriate and potentially dangerous invasion of her privacy.

One thing I've learned is that when clergypersons cross a boundary of misconduct of any kind, they have usually crossed many other, less egregious ones along the way before that, setting up a climate for acceptance of behavior. Likewise when parishioners know no boundaries in regards to the personal lives of clergywomen, they are also more likely to set up an environment where someone can take advantage of the fact that no one will believe, help or advocate for the clergywoman.

If it's okay to make personal comments (on hair, dress, or size), and ask personal questions (about dating, marriage, or having children), then it is more likely that an environment will be created that encourages and supports (tacitly or openly) increasing levels of sexual harassment, such as stalking, assault or rape. Obviously not everyone who crosses these boundaries violates the more egregious ones, but those who prey on others may find an accepting context in which to fulfill their own needs and women are placed in an uncomfortable or even dangerous situation.

I know that clergymen are often the source of their parishioners' pursuant interest in their personal lives, especially if they are single, but clergywomen are markedly more vulnerable on many levels. In addition to often being physically more vulnerable, she may be less powerful in her relationships within the church than a clergyman would be. The imbalance of power for a clergywoman is evident when a male leader in the church who might not be pleased to have a clergywoman or disagrees with her leadership may use such tactics as "seemingly harmless flirtation" to demean or confuse her and others. If she objects or tactfully tries to address such a situation, she can be subjected to further humiliation if he turns on her and spreads rumors. Who will they believe? Will it be the clergywoman or the long-time member, family member or powerful member of the community?

Since there is still a tenuous acceptance of clergywomen in many churches today, a clergywoman who objects or sets boundaries about her personal life is much more likely to upset the congregation in such a way that her appointment is jeopardized.

That raises another point. At least in The United Methodist Church, there are no significant consequences for bad behavior by laity. A church or its clergyperson cannot "excommunicate" a member—and I'm not sure that I would want to go in that direction without some careful thought—but likewise there is no mechanism that holds a layperson accountable for bad behavior of any kind in a local church.

I was surprised to learn in this book that there had been a recent trial for a lay member of the United Methodist Church. Frustrated district superintendents and other angry parishioners occasionally ask if they can make a complaint against a layperson. I personally have sought to avoid this action for many reasons, but mostly because even if it were to go to a trial that ruled against the layperson, how is a layperson held accountable?

When lay people have acted inappropriately toward each other or toward a clergyperson, the best I have been able to do is work toward an agreement of behavior. If need be, given the severity of the situation, the only resort to the breaking of the behavioral covenant is to involve the civil authorities. Even if it is best for the clergywoman to be moved to another community for her safety and well-being, it leaves a church with a layperson who is an abuser of clergy (or other vulnerable people) in their midst.

So what can we do?

This book calls us to raise awareness about the vulnerability of clergywomen. Some specific actions that can be taken include:

- Find a safe way for clergywomen to share their experiences of sexual harassment. Church leaders—district superintendents and bishops, both male and female—may be surprised at the depth and breadth of the experience.

- Begin to develop resources and training for laity on all matters of healthy and respectful behavior within the life of the church, including civil or holy conversation in the midst of disagreement or dissatisfaction, respect for all people in the congregation, the expectation that the clergy will be treated respectfully even if there is conflict with her or him, and clearer expectations about inquiring into the personal life of the clergy and violating the privacy of the clergy. For instance, trustees need to be reminded that they can't just come and go into the parsonage. The well-meaning Bible study members need to be taught that they should to be respectful of the personal life of the pastor, inquiring only when invited to do so by information given to them from the pastor herself. These and many other specific ways of being respectful of clergy are needed today in a climate that has invaded the church where people believe that they can say or do anything toward the clergy.

- Clear, supportive and detailed behavioral covenants need to be made with the assistance of the district superintendent when there are physical, emotional and relational violations against the privacy and person of the clergywoman. Included in those covenants may need to be the expectation that if certain behaviors are violated, the civil authorities will be called.

- Clergy boundary training needs to include training for clergywomen that helps them establish clear boundaries from the very beginning for their own well-being and specifically what to do if they feel their boundaries are being violated by laity, other clergy, the district superintendent or bishop. They also need training on how to take care of themselves when they feel physically vulnerable.

If someone is violating the clergywoman's boundaries, chances are good that this person has violated in the past or is presently violating someone else's boundaries within the church, community or even family. Careful attention should be given to others who may be in a vulnerable position around the perpetrator.

This book is a great start in raising awareness. I trust that it will begin conversations among clergywomen across the church and also with judicatory leaders who may or may not be aware or sensitive to the level of harassment that clergywomen experience. I hope that these issues will be raised in annual conferences so that there is a greater sense of awareness and sensitivity.

The one thing we can all do is raise this concern whenever we are discussing boundaries with clergy. Just mentioning it may help a woman come forward with a situation of harassment in her life that can be addressed if she feels like someone may help.

I sent a letter explaining my concerns to the popular storyteller that has made Minnesota famous. Several weeks later, just before publication of this book, he had a short segment that described Pastor Liz coming into the cafe in the mythical town following her vacation to a totally different place than described a few weeks earlier. I thought that odd but it got better! She sat down next to the storyteller in his own mythical town with an assertive air about her. She said, "You've been talking about me!" She told him that she had not crawled up on the bed beside a dying man. The storyteller said to Pastor Liz, "That's what I was told!" She said it wasn't true; that he had asked her to but she didn't do it. She went on in an assertive way, telling him to watch himself (and that he should stop picking on the Lutherans!).

I don't know if it was my letter or a deluge of complaints that caused this story teller to "fix" the depiction of Pastor Liz but it only goes to show that change is possible when we make people aware. I also like where the story is going with such an assertive Pastor Liz!

Clergywomen are "under the stained glass ceiling," an image that suggests limitations and restrictions, specifically those created by the lack of boundaries on the part of laity that give rise to fear, intimidation, and humiliation. The image of stained glass reminds me of so many churches, big and small. In churches across the country and The United Methodist Church, behind stained glass windows there has been both violence and the bright light of hope that Jesus gives to the world outside and the church inside.

After the 1963 bombing of the Sixteenth Avenue Baptist Church in Birmingham, Alabama, the only window that remained intact was one of the familiar image of Jesus knocking on the door. While the window was intact, the face of Jesus was destroyed. Violence of any kind destroys the face of Jesus for the world and the church. Because there is violence, we must talk about these issues and make changes in our hearts and practices so that we can become the face of Jesus for the world outside and the church inside.

Yet another church commissioned stained glass windows of Jesus and the disciples with children, women and men on the hills of Galilee. But none of the figures had eyes. When the windows were dedicated, the congregation pledged to be the eyes of Jesus and his disciples as they watched over and cared for the children, women and men in their church and community.

Our witness is like the light that shines through our stained glass windows from the inside out. Whose face and eyes does the world see? Whose face and eyes do clergywomen and others who are vulnerable to sexual harassment see?

Let God's light shine through us to the world and the church!

Our Covenant for Zero Tolerance

We, the people of The United Methodist Church, covenant with each other to create a safety net within United Methodism for the care and nurture of all.

The United Methodist Church calls all persons to reject sexual misconduct, gender and sexual harassment and inappropriateness in every form toward any clergy, members, or any person. We do not tolerate gender or sexual harassment in any form: inappropriateness, sexual jokes and gestures, gender stereotyping comments, or refusal to accept leadership on account of gender.

We expect pastors, teachers, leaders, members and constituents in the church to model and teach appropriate behavior. We covenant to do no harm to others.

By this covenant we declare that we will not engage in sexual misconduct, child abuse, sexual or gender harassment, or behaviors that undermine the Gospel and the ministries of The United Methodist Church.

This covenant is designed to be posted in every church facility, to be published annually in print and used on websites.

Church Conduct Policy

Inappropriate Actions

Sexual harassment.
Any unwanted touch or sexual contact, gesture or innuendo.
Sexual misconduct, assault, or rape.
Name calling.
Putdowns, insults, or bullying.
Gossip.
Threatening, manipulating, or intimating behavior.
Damaging property, stealing or harming persons.
Stalking.
Entering church property or the pastor's home without invitation.

Recognizing Inappropriate Words and Body Language

1. When touch doesn't feel good.
2. When words are spoken with sexual meanings.
3. When body language or words are threatening.
4. When a person is singled out for sexual behavior.
5. When people are shunned or ignored.
6. When behavior impedes the work of a pastor or the church.
7. When someone exposes private body parts.

This policy is designed to be posted in every church facility, to be published annually in print and used on websites.

Conduct Policy for Children

Our Safe Conduct Rules

1. Don't hurt anyone.
2. Don't call people names.
3. Don't hurt, destroy or take what belongs to someone else.
4. Don't insult people.
5. Don't say bad things about other people.
6. Don't follow people to make them afraid.
7. Don't go with strangers.

Tell a Safe Adult About a Problem

1. If someone touches you and it doesn't feel right.
2. If you don't feel good where you are.
3. If what people say about you doesn't feel right.
4. If you are being bullied.
5. If someone makes you feel ashamed.
6. If someone makes you feel uncomfortable.
7. If people ignore you.
8. If you don't feel safe.

This policy is designed to be posted in every church facility serving children and youth, to be published annually in print and used on websites.

Bibliography

Anna Howard Shaw Center. "2010 Study of Retention of United Methodist Clergywomen." Boston, MA. This study has not been released as of the date of publication of this book.

Avis, Paul. *Authority, Leadership and Conflict in the Church.* Philadelphia, PA: Trinity Press International, 1992.

"Avoiding Gender Bias." Kansas National Education Association. www.knea.org/aboutknea/index.html. Accessed 10, October 2010.

Banyei, Candace R. *Understanding Clergy Misconduct in Religious Systems: Scapegoating, Family Secrets, and the Abuse of Power.* New York: Haworth Pastoral Press, 1998.

Becker, Carol E. *Leading Women: How Church Women Can Avoid Leadership Traps and Negotiate the Gender Maze.* Nashville, TN: Abingdon Press, 1996.

Bick, E. Wilbur. "Female Clergy: A Case of Professional Marginality." *The American Journal of Sociology,* 72:5. March 1967.

"Bike Photo of Bishop Swenson Undignified." *Circuit West,* California-Pacific Annual Conference, The United Methodist Church. November 2006.

Boers, Arthur Paul. *Never Call Them Jerks.* Washington, DC: Alban Institute, 2002.

Brekus, Catherine A. *Strangers and Pilgrims: Female Preaching in America, 1740-1845*. Chapel Hill, NC: The University of North Carolina, 1998.

Buttry, Daniel. *Bringing Your Church Back to Life: Beyond Survival Mentality*. Valley Forge, PA: Judson Press, 1988.

Chaves, Mark. *Ordaining Women*. Cambridge MS: Harvard University Press, 1997.

Chilcote, Paul Wesley, *John Wesley and the Women Preachers of Early Methodism*. London: Scarecrow Press, 1991.

Conroy, John. *Unspeakable Acts, Ordinary People: The Dynamics of Torture*. Berkeley, CA: University of California Press, 2000.

Cosgrove, Charles H. and Dennis D. Hatfield. *Church Conflict*. Nashville, TN: Abingdon Press, 1994.

Cooper, Beth, "Survey of Clergywomen and Sexual Harassment in The United Methodist Church," San Diego, CA: 2003.

Cooper, Beth. "Do No Harm: Sexual Harassment by Laity of United Methodist Clergywomen by Laity." D. Min. Dissertation, Wesley Theological Seminary, 2007.

"Domestic Violence Fact Sheet." U.S. Department of Justice National Crime Victimization Survey, 1996. www.athealth.com/consumer/disorders/DomViolFacts.html. Updated 29 December, 2009. Accessed 24 October, 2010.

Eradication of Sexual Harassment, http:www.gcsrw.org/EradicationofSexualHarassment.aspx. Accessed 24 October, 2010.

Federal Bureau of Investigation, Crime Statistics. www.fbi.gov. Accessed 14 April, 2007.

"Female Clergy Are the Target of Harassment." *Toronto Star*. March 13, 1994.

Fortune, Marie Marshall. *Sexual Violence, The Unmentionable Sin: An Ethical and Pastoral Perspective*. New York: The Pilgrim Press, 1983.

Foucault, Michael. *Power/ Knowledge: Selected Interviews and other Writings*. New York: Pantheon Books, 1980.

Frank, Thomas Edward. *Polity, Preaching and the Mission of The United Methodist Church*. Nashville, TN: Abingdon Press, 1997.

Gordon, Colin, ed. *Power/Knowledge: Selected Interviews and Other Writings*. New York: Pantheon Books, 1980.

Gorham, Leta and Thomas W. Waitschies. *But They Won't Talk to a Woman*. New York, NY: University Press of America, 1998.

Hefling, Kimberly. "Veterans File Abuse Suit Against Comrades." *The Post and Courier,* Charleston, SC. February 16, 2011.

Howe, Margaret E. *Women and Church Leadership*. Grand Rapids, MI: Zondervan Press, 1982.

Ice, Martha Long. *Clergywomen and Their Views: Calling for a new Age*. New York, NY: Praegar, Inc., 1987.

Katzenstein, Mary Fainsod. *Faithful and Fearless: Moving Feminist Protest Inside the Church and Military*. Princeton, NJ: Princeton University Press, 1998.

Leontine Kelly. Presentation to the Holy Boldness Convocation, an Urban Ministries Conference of The United Methodist Church. San Francisco, CA. 23 November, 1997.

Landau, Elaine. *Sexual Harassment*. New York: Walker and Company, 1993.

Legacqz, Karen and Ronald Barton. *Sex in the Parish*. Louisville, KY: Westminster/John Knox Press, 1991.

Lebacqz, Karen and Joseph D. Driskill. *Ethics and Spiritual Care*. Nashville, TN: Abingdon Press, 2000.

Lehman, Edward Jr. *Breaking Through Gender Barriers*. Princeton, NJ: Transaction Press, 1985.

MacKinnon, Catherine. *Sexual Harassment of Working Women*. New Haven, CT: Yale University Press, 1979.

"Many Female Clergy Still Face a Stained-Glass Ceiling." *Fort Worth Star*. 17 July, 1999.

Martin, Frank. *War in the Pews: A Foxhole Guide to Surviving Church Conflict*. Downers Grove, IL: Intervarsity Press, 1995.

McCall Tigert, Leanne. *Coming Out Through Fire: Surviving the Trauma of Homophobia*. Cleveland, OH: United Church Press, 1999.

McClintock, Karen. *Sexual Shame, An Urgent Call to Healing*. Minneapolis, MN: Augsburg Fortress Press, 2001.

Murphy-Geiss, Gail. "Sexual harassment in The United Methodist Church, 2005." Chicago, IL: The General Commission on the Status and Role of Women, The United Methodist Church, 2005.

Nesbitt, Paula D. *Feminization of the Clergy in America: Occupational and Organizational Perspectives*. New York, NY: Oxford University Press, 1997.

New York Times, August 26, 2006, 11.

"Number of Clergywomen in Annual Conferences." www.gcfa.org/PDFs/Gender2004.pdf. Accessed 5 November, 2006.

"Stained Glass Ceiling Affect for Clergywomen." *New York Times*. 26 August, 2006.

Rediger, G. Lloyd. *Clergy Killers*. Louisville, KY: Westminster/John Knox Press, 1997.

Reilly, Patricia Lynn. *A God Who Looks Like Me*. New York, NY: Balantine Books, 1995.

Rich, Adrienne. *Blood, Bread, and Poetry: Selected Prose, 1979-1985*. New York, NY: Norton Co, 1999.

Richards, David A. J. *Women, Gays and the Constitution: The Grounds for Feminism and Gay Rights in Culture and Law*. Chicago, IL: University of Chicago Press, 1998.

Richardson, Ronald. *Creating a Healthier Church*. Minneapolis, MI: Fortress Press, 1996.

Richardson, Ronald. *Family Ties that Bind*. Bellingham, WA: Sell-Council Press, 1995.

Ross, Susan Deller and others. *The Rights of Women*. Champagne, IL: Southern Illinois Press, 1993.

Saguay, Abigail C. *What Is Sexual Harassment?* Berkeley, CA: University of California Press, 2003.

Schaef, Ann Wilson and Diane Fassell. *The Addictive Organization*. Lanham, MD: The University Press of America, Inc., 1998.

Schmidt, K. Louise. *Transforming Abuse: Nonviolent Resistance and Recovery*. Philadelphia, PA: New Society Publisher, 1995.

Schüssler Fiorenza, Elisabeth. *Discipleship of Equals*. New York, NY: Crossroads, 1993.

Scrimgeour,Ron. "Gender bias in the Classroom?" *Research Education* 52, Spring, 1993. www.scre.ac.uk/rie/n152scrimgeour.html. Accessed 6 April 2007.

"Sex Lawsuits Force Change in Churches." *Denver Post*. 1 May, 1994.

"Sexual Ethics Policy for Clergy of the Oregon Idaho Annual Conference of The United Methodist Church," 2008.

Shaw, Anna Howard. *The Story of a Pioneer*. Cleveland, OH: The Pilgrim Press, 1994.

Shawchuck, Norman, and Roger Heuser. *Managing the Congregation: Building Effective Systems to Serve People*. Nashville, TN: Abingdon Press, 1996.

Shehan, Constance, and Marsha Wiggens Frame. "1995 Survey of 190 Ordained United Methodist Clergywomen." University of Colorado, Denver, CO. http: //news. ufl. edu/1999/06/09/clergy. Accessed 12 October 2006.

Smith, Christine. *Preaching as Weeping, Confession and Resistance*. Louisville, KY: Westminster/John Knox Press, 1992.

Steinke, Peter L. *How Your Church Family Works*. New York, NY: Alban Institute, 1996.

Telushkin, Joseph. *Words that Hurt, Words that Heal*. New York, NY: Quill William Morrow, 1996.

The Relay Online, email newsletter of the Greater New Jersey Conference of The United Methodist Church, May 2009, 5. UMRelay.org. Not accessible, 2 February, 2011.

"The Sexual Harassment of Clergywomen." *Boston Globe*. 12 November, 2000.

The United Methodist Church. *The Book of Discipline of The United Methodist Church.* Nashville, TN: United Methodist Publishing House, 2000, 2004, 2008.

The United Methodist Church. *The Book of Resolutions of The United Methodist Church.* Nashville, TN: United Methodist Publishing House, 2000, 2004, 2008.

Thoele, Sue Patton. *The Courage to Be Yourself: A Woman's Guide to Growing Beyond Emotional Dependence.* Berkeley, CA: Conari Press, 1991.

Thompson, Patricia J. *Courageous Past, Bold Future.* Nashville, TN: General Board of Higher Education, 2006.

Tressler, Phyllis. *Woman's Inhumanity to Woman.* New York, NY: Plume, 2002.

Trickett, David. Letter to Alumni. Denver, CO: The Iliff School of Theology. 8 November, 2010.

"UF Study: Female Ministers face Pettiness, Patriarchy and Pressure." Filed 9 June, 1999. http://www.news.ufl.edu/1999/06/09/clergy. Accessed 30 November, 2010.

White, Vern. *A Call to Hope: Living as Christians in a Violent Society.* New York, NY: Friendship Press, 1997.

Willard, Frances E. *Woman in the Pulpit.* 1888. Reprint, Washington, DC: Zenger Publishing Co. 1978.

Winter, Miriam Therese, Adiar Lummis, and Allison Strokes, *Defecting in Place; Women Claiming Responsibility for Their Own Spiritual Lives.* New York: Crossroad, 1994.

"Women Clergy Face Barriers in Male-Dominated Churches." *Palm Beach Post.* 25 July, 1999.

Zikmund, Barbara Brown, Adair T. Lummis, Patricia M. Y. Yang. *Clergy Women: An Uphill Calling.* Louisville, KY: Westminster/John Knox Press, 1998.

Interviews

Anonymous. Interview 1 with author. 16 June, 2001. San Diego, CA. Interview in person, notes.

Anonymous. Interview 2 with author. 6 November, 2001. San Diego, CA. Interview in person, notes.

Anonymous. Interview 3 with author. 12 January 2001. San Diego, CA. Telephone interview, notes.

Anonymous. Interview 7 with author. 8 January 2003. San Diego, CA. Interview in person, notes.

Anonymous. Interview 9 with author. June 2001, San Diego, CA. Personal interview, notes.

Anonymous. Interview 79 with author. 10 March 2003. San Diego, CA. Telephone interview, notes.

Anonymous. Interview 191with author. 14 May 2004. San Diego, CA. Personal interview, notes.

Anonymous. Interview 312 with author. 28 November 2006. San Diego, CA. Telephone interview, notes.

Available from
Frontrowliving Press

www.frontrowliving.com
PO Box 19291
San Diego, CA 92159
frontrowliving@yahoo.com

Under the Stained Glass Ceiling: Sexual Harassment of United Methodist Clergywomen   by Beth A. Cooper $17.95

Discounts are available on bulk orders.

Join the conversation on *facebook* at
Under The Stained Glass Ceiling.

Read stories and share yours at
www.underthestainedglassceiling.com

The Rev. Dr. Beth A. Cooper is a United Methodist elder. For over twenty years she has served local churches and campus ministries. She is a graduate of Duquesne University with a Bachelor of Music in voice performance; Perkins School of Theology, Southern Methodist University, with Master of Sacred Music and Master of Divinity degrees; and Wesley Theological Seminary, with a Doctorate in Ministry. She also received a Graduate Certificate in Women's Studies from San Diego State University. In 2010, Cooper received the Duquesne University with the Mind, Heart and Spirit Award for Moral and Spiritual Values for her work in ministry.

NOTES

www.ingramcontent.com/pod-product-compliance
Lightning Source LLC
Chambersburg PA
CBHW072251270326
41930CB00010B/2351